"'Any time hell launches a plan against you, it is a criminal act.' What a profound statement! Dr. Alston proceeds to describe in detail what this means and the corresponding action we should take. This book is chock-full of critical insights and essential interventions to nullify the fallout from spiritual criminal acts. I found the book fresh, engaging and very helpful in explaining how to overcome. Great book and worth the read!"

—Barbara J. Yoder, lead apostle, Shekinah Regional Apostolic Center and Breakthrough Apostolic Ministries Network

"*Next-Level Spiritual Warfare* is a powerful book that provokes believers with the understanding that spiritual ignorance is not to be tolerated. Venner Alston releases strategic revelation concerning principalities and powers, familial spirits and other hindrances to prayer. Every believer needs this book in their library!"

—Barbara Wentroble, president, International Breakthrough Ministries and Breakthrough Business Leaders

"Believers are given spiritual weapons to defeat the kingdom of darkness through effective, power-packed warfare prayer. Venner Alston's insightful book, *Next-Level Spiritual Warfare*, takes believers up the revelatory ladder into the next dimension to learn the principles of persistent prayer that empower them to experience heaven's answers and breakthroughs."

—Dr. Barbie L. Breathitt, founder, Breath of the Spirit Ministries

"Spiritual warfare is a reality that all believers deal with in our lives, cities and regions. It is vital to have strong, wise and scriptural instruction on how to engage in effective warfare. As you journey through this book, you will be powerfully equipped to understand the enemy's tactics, and you will most definitely receive impartation and revelation about the awesome Kingdom inheritance that God has bestowed on each of us. Knowledge builds power for action. Be awakened to become the fearless and bold warrior you are destined to be."

—Rebecca Greenwood, co-founder, Christian Harvest International and Strategic Prayer Apostolic Network; author, *Defeating Strongholds of the Mind*

"You've prayed and believed God, yet there seems to be no answer. Could it be that the problem is not your faith, it's your *fight*? You have an adversary! And in this revelatory book, Venner Alston teaches us how to win the war in the heavens so that we can experience the manifestation in the earth."

—Isaac Pitre, founder, Isaac Pitre Ministries

"This is a great, easy to read and useful handbook for living and praying effectively in the Kingdom. It teaches practical ways to open the pathways of God's blessings in our lives as well as how to overcome the enemy."

—Kent Mattox, founder, Word Alive International Outreach

Next-Level SpirituaL WARFARE

Advanced Strategies *for* Defeating *the* Enemy

VENNER J. ALSTON

Chosen

a division of Baker Publishing Group
Minneapolis, Minnesota

Published by Chosen Books
11400 Hampshire Avenue South
Bloomington, Minnesota 55438
www.chosenbooks.com

Chosen Books is a division of
Baker Publishing Group, Grand Rapids, Michigan

Printed in the United States of America

Library of Congress Cataloging-in-Publication Data
Names: Alston, Venner J., author.
Title: Next-level spiritual warfare : advanced strategies for defeating the enemy / Venner J. Alston.
Description: Minneapolis : Chosen, a division of Baker Publishing Group, 2019. | Includes bibliographical references.
Identifiers: LCCN 2018053592 | ISBN 9780800799281 (trade paper) | ISBN 9781493418831 (e-book)
Subjects: LCSH: Spiritual warfare.
Classification: LCC BV4509.5 .A47 2019 | DDC 235/.4—dc23
LC record available at https://lccn.loc.gov/2018053592

20   21   22   23   24   25   8   7   6   5   4

I dedicate this book to my late husband,
Apostle Bill Alston, my greatest supporter and champion,
and to my circle of prayer warriors,
who encouraged and prayed for me throughout this project.

Contents

Foreword

There is such a war over establishing God's Kingdom plan on earth. Because of what we are warring against, we must have an effective prayer strategy. In the late 1970s, the Lord began to move in me to renew and energize my prayer life. I found myself staying up late and praying. God gave me actual prayer assignments. He had me pray for individuals, for my Sunday school class, for our church, for my pastor and for the church staff. I prayed for the company at which I worked. I prayed for my family. I was simply enjoying communicating with the Lord and watching Him work.

One night, after I had my prayer time, I was awakened at 2:00 a.m., and our dog was growling and getting into the bed with us. My wife, Pam, was awakened and startled as well. I felt a presence at the end of our bed. Pam described this presence as a slimy green vapor. I stood up on our bed and commanded this presence to leave our house. I knew that the enemy was angry over my prayer life becoming active. It was as if he was attempting to produce fear in me so I would stop praying. He knew that if I kept seeking the Lord with all my heart I would eventually be free and able to recognize and confront him in new ways to defeat his purposes.

We must never let the enemy create fear in us, nor be afraid of understanding the enemy's schemes, character and ways. That is why I am so excited about this book. In *Next-Level Spiritual Warfare*, Dr. Venner Alston provides foundational principles that will help you and others become more effective in praying and experiencing answers to your prayers. This resource will help you rise up and turn back the battle at the gates.

A Time to War

Christians must learn why it is imperative that we fight and overturn the plans of the enemy. Learning to war comes easier to some than to others. For those who grew up in relative peace and comfort, it may come hardest of all. "Why is war necessary? Why can people not live in harmony?" These are the questions we ask our parents when we are first exposed to conflict. We ask questions of our history teachers when we learn the events that brought us to the present. Most importantly, we ask questions of God. "If you are a loving God, why do war and destruction occur?" The short answer is that we are called to serve in God's army of warriors. If we do not heed His call, then the enemy will step in, and he will rule in our stead. We are called to possess, secure and protect our inheritance. We must remember that the earth is the Lord's and the fullness thereof!

As the Holy Spirit moves us toward becoming more Christlike, the methodology of an old season will not propel us into the future. This is one of the wiles of the enemy—to hold us captive in the last manifestation of God. We live in the past rather than move into the best that is ahead for our life. We need something new and fresh. We need a new glory.

When we are moving in God's glory, angelic visitation occurs. In December 2017, I was chosen by the Lord for an angelic visitation. We must collaborate with the host of heaven when we are moving in the glory realm in the earth. We are the army of earth. The host of heaven interact with us to bring God's victory into the earth realm.

The angel from my visitation was peering into the harvest throughout the earth. I entered into what he was seeing, but neither space nor time permits me to share all of it here. When I asked him what his name was, he said, *"I am the angel of war over God's covenant harvest plan."* He revealed to me the harvest shift that we would enter and how this is a time for us to break out of conventional ways of thinking. We must make a "harvest shift" and be led through the gate of harvest increase. There will be a great hardening, separation and sharpening! This will draw out the army order of the present Body . . . and be the first harvest training! This angel took me through several other steps of training that we will go through in the future.

- Grace will be sovereignly extended for wrong alignments in past covenants (Hagars, Ishmaels, brothers and sisters who persecuted you, Esaus and Marks). This will be the second harvest training!
- Saints' eyes will be opened to the carrion scavengers that have ravished their covenant plan (your bloodline and mission). This will be the third harvest training!
- New angelic councils will be forming and assigned to territories. These teams will meet with apostolic-prophetic councils in the earth realm to give strategies for advancement. This will be the fourth harvest training!
- The desire of nations will be for God to reveal Himself! Public decrees will be heard from civil leaders who will call entire territories and peoples into awakening. This will be the fifth harvest training!

- God's people will be sorted by their gleaning faithfulness. This will give them *reaping* access. This will be the sixth harvest training!
- The territorial threshing floors for the harvest will be revealed! New calls to harvesters will be extended. This will be the seventh harvest training!

God has a government. He is Lord Sabaoth, "The God of Hosts." He has an army in heaven, and He aligns that host with His Kingdom army in the earth. He has angels and saints coming together to advance the Kingdom. Dr. Alston is one of God's generals who is educating the Body of Christ with new strategies. *Next-Level Spiritual Warfare* reveals the corporate weapons for our warfare and divine decrees on how to use them when we engage in the battlefields of the future. As you read this book, I am praying you will become connected to God's Spirit of wisdom and revelation so that you will have every strategy needed to defeat the devil in your life, family, territory and every sphere of influence you have stewardship over.

Dr. Chuck D. Pierce, president, Global Spheres, Inc.;
president, Glory of Zion International Ministries

Introduction

When I was a new believer, prayer, fasting and a consistent habit of studying the Word of God were carefully woven into my spiritual foundation. I learned to *pray*. My church had experienced a sudden harvest of believers between the ages of 18 and 25, and the church leaders had their hands full trying to disciple young people who were added weekly in large numbers for six months. The leaders understood the power and importance of prayer; they knew this was the key not only to retaining the harvest but also to seeing a generation take its place in the Body of Christ. One of their primary objectives was to ensure that the new believers would fulfill their God-given destinies, chosen for each of them in his or her mother's womb.

In these early days of my faith, it was my custom to spend long periods of time on my knees in prayer before God. I was unemployed and unmarried, and I had the privilege of having the freedom to set aside long blocks of time for prayer and reading the Word of God. Our church regularly engaged in corporate fasting and prayer at least one weekend per month. This was in addition to our weekly Tuesday and Friday fast days. Regular attendance at church meetings was encouraged, which, for the first two years of my Christian life, meant seven days a week and twice on Sundays. (This schedule changed after those two years.) Systematic teaching from the Word of God, prayer and deliverance were a consistent part of these gatherings. Our instruction in the dynamics of victorious Christian living was to be marked by prayer and fasting.

To help us transition into Kingdom living, we attended meetings called shut-ins. These were intense times of prayer beginning on Friday evening and ending on Sunday morning at 6:00 a.m. As the term *shut-in* suggests, everyone remained at the church during that time, taking only short breaks to freshen up. We also observed a water fast. Sleeping was not part of the agenda (although we were known to take brief naps). We came in on Friday evening and did not leave until early Sunday morning; afterward we left for home to prepare for the Sunday morning worship gathering. These times of fervent prayer marked me in a way that continues today. We experienced the power of God in remarkable ways; healings and baptisms in the Holy Spirit were common during these gatherings.

As a new believer who was learning how to pray, I noticed one thing that stood out about these times of prayer. People in the church would often close their prayers with the statement, "If it is God's will, I will receive what I have asked the Lord for." It seemed that even though they were praying in the name of Jesus, they questioned whether their prayers were legitimate requests. Is it possible that their requests were in God's will, yet they would not receive a response? How do we reconcile delayed responses with prayers that we know are in God's will?

As young believers, we were taught that God responds to prayers in three ways: yes, no and not yet. Delayed responses were then perceived as God either saying, "No" or "Not yet." While I agree that these are possible explanations for delayed responses to prayers, I would like to propose another reason: Could it be that delayed responses to our prayers are the result of hindrances sent against our prayers by the kingdom of darkness? Could it be that many prayer requests are granted by God, and hell delays the response? I know for some of you this is quite a challenging premise. If we believe, however, that we have an adversary who goes about as a roaring lion, we must believe that a key strategy of this adversary is to hinder our prayers. When our prayers are unanswered, hell tries to influence our thought processes and move us from faith to doubt by whispering, "Has God really said?" or "God answers the prayers of everyone else, but He does not answer yours." It is at this moment that discouragement can set in and convince us to stop praying and believe that God does not respond to our prayers.

The Word of God commands us to pray without ceasing. Prayer is when we commune with God. Through prayer we also petition God for our needs or other requests. Scripture encourages us to ask our heavenly Father for the things we need: "Ask and keep on asking and it will be given to you; seek and keep on seeking and you will find; knock and keep on knocking and the door will be opened to you" (Matthew 7:7 AMP).

This Scripture provides some insights concerning prayer. The instruction is to *ask and keep on asking, seek and keep on seeking, knock and keep on knocking.* This implies an attitude of persistence. One of the most important disciplines believers must develop is the discipline of prayer. Prayerlessness does not lead you to the place of victory. Prayerlessness leads to defeat. It does not strengthen you as an overcomer in Christ. It results in being overcome as you battle the enemy of your soul. When we know that our requests are in God's will, unanswered prayers are not satisfactory. Since we are encouraged not only to ask but to seek and knock in prayer, should we not then expect responses to our prayers?

APPLICATION

One of the most important disciplines believers must develop is the discipline of prayer.

Communing with God in prayer is a characteristic of a healthy Christian life. It is most frequently referred to as devotional prayer. During devotional prayer, we learn to hear the voice of God. Incredible worship arises in us as God reveals His character and nature. Great strength is imparted as we commune with God. Although devotional prayer is an essential aspect of the believer's life, it is not the subject of this book. In these pages we will discover hidden truths concerning a dimension of prayer most often referred to as warfare prayer.

Many believers approach prayer from a passive position, thinking they need not do anything other than to ask once and wait. But we must *keep on asking*, *keep on seeking*, and *keep on knocking*. This book is intended to be a guide for engagement in strong, militant prayer that will help you to partner with heaven to see more of your prayers answered. As you read, you will discover how to pray more effectively and move your life forward. We have been called to rule on earth. This means that we walk in dominion and exercise Kingdom rulership:

> And God blessed them, and God said unto them, "Be fruitful and multiply, and replenish the earth, and subdue it; and have dominion over the fish of the sea, and over the fowl of the air, and over every living thing that moveth upon the earth."
>
> Genesis 1:28

Warfare prayer is praying in the midst of our spiritual battles. Christians have an enemy in Satan and his demons (see Ephesians 6:12), and prayer is commanded in the context of putting on the armor of God (see verse 18). Warfare prayer does not mean praying harder, praying more decisively or assuming authority we do not have. It means praying according to Scripture, trusting in the power of God and submitting our will to His. Warfare prayer is using the spiritual weapons of faith to overturn unrighteous edicts that have been written against us by the powers of darkness. "We live in this world, but we don't fight our battles in the same way the world does. The weapons we use are not human ones. Our weapons have power from God and can destroy the enemy's strong places" (2 Corinthians 10:3–4 ERV).

God has given spiritual weapons to believers to war against the kingdom of darkness. Not only that, we do not fight alone. All of the resources of heaven are available to us to ensure our victory as we war in faith, trusting in the finished work of Christ. Our weapons are not human in nature; our weapons are supernatural. God gives us supernatural ability to overthrow the powers of darkness that are hindering our prayers. The might of heaven is released on our behalf when we pray in faith. Ministering angels are assigned to each of us, the heirs of salvation. Think about this for a moment. When you pray, angelic forces are released on your behalf! "And concerning the angels He says, 'Who makes His angels winds, and His ministering servants flames of fire [to do His bidding]'" (Hebrews 1:7 AMP).

God does not stand back and leave you to engage the spiritual realm alone. He has armed you with every weapon you need to overcome the powers of darkness. He sends His angelic forces to war alongside you on your behalf. You have the power of His Word and the finished work of Christ in your arsenal. When you use these powerful weapons, the enemy must bow. Any demonic force holding your goods, which are your inheritance, must let go.

We are commanded to pray in faith and not waver or doubt. Could there be a dimension of prayer that Christians have overlooked or neglected? Could it be that there are hindrances to prayer that must be overcome? Is it possible for the kingdom of darkness to hinder responses to our prayers? We must learn how to become consistent in prayer, to continue asking until our prayers are answered. Far too many believers fail to receive a response to their prayers and settle for less than what God has planned for their lives. The reality is that effective prayer works. Dr. C. Peter Wagner wrote,

> Not all prayer works, but *effective* prayer does. *Powerful* prayer works. . . . Not all prayer is equal. Just as some prayer is effective, so some is ineffective, and some is in between. Just as some prayer is powerful, so, unfortunately, some is equally impotent.[1]

This book will provide principles to help you and others become more effective in praying and experiencing answers to your prayers. As you experience answers to prayers, you become more encouraged to pray. Not receiving answers to your prayers is much like having a phone conversation with someone in which you are the only person engaged in the conversation, or in which the other person makes promises that are not fulfilled. That is not who God is. He is faithful and true. God told Jeremiah, "I will hasten My word to perform it" (Jeremiah 1:12). If indeed Christ is the same yesterday, today and forever (see Hebrews 13:8), then we can no longer settle for not receiving answers to our prayers. I encourage you to meditate on the truths set forth in this book and allow Holy Spirit to illuminate revelation to help you to rise and engage heaven in a way that you see more answers to your prayers.

CHAPTER ONE

What Just Happened?

A thief has only one thing in mind—he wants to steal, slaughter, and destroy. But I have come to give you everything in abundance, more than you expect—life in its fullness until you overflow!

John 10:10 TPT

Some years ago, after spending time in prayer, I felt the prompting of the Holy Spirit to host a women's conference. I was a bit apprehensive about this assignment and decided to spend more time in prayer over it. Again I felt the impression of Holy Spirit to host a women's conference. So I assembled a team, and we began implementing the practical aspects of conference hosting.

Registration was going well, and I was excited about the upcoming gathering. A month before the conference was to commence, I had a dream in which I could see myself in an airplane. The altitude was good as we moved forward. All of a sudden, the telephone towers started growing. Not only were the towers growing, but the communication lines attached to them were also growing. We were trying to avoid hitting the wires but could not. I awakened wondering what the dream meant.

Two days later, I was informed that registration had come to a screeching halt. No one was registering. We increased our prayer efforts for the meeting, but nothing changed. We had contracted to host the meeting at a local hotel, so we could not cancel without incurring financial penalties. Hoping that registrations at the door would multiply, we continued planning, but it did not happen. We ended up with fewer registrations than we needed to meet the budget. The thief had come against us, stealing the increase that God had purposed for us.

I could not understand what had happened. I had had a clear word from the Lord, but here I was, defeated in this effort. I have talked to many leaders who have had similar experiences. What happens when you have a clear word from the Lord and yet failure happens?

I wish I could tell you that I figured out what happened and recovered quickly, and that every subsequent event was successful. Unfortunately, a cycle of failure had been activated that repeated for several years. It appeared that I was unable to progress in ministry. I seemed to be locked in a pattern of experiencing less than God had revealed to me during times of prayer or prophetic ministry. I knew these limitations had not come from the Lord; success was God's plan for me, just as it had been for Jeremiah. But I did not know how to move beyond this point. I did not know how to break out of the cycle of defeat. I felt trapped on the borders of breakthrough and unable to cross over fully into God's promises. I prayed and mobilized intercessors, yet God's promises concerning success in ministry did not seem to manifest.

Perhaps you are experiencing some of these same issues. What has God spoken about that you have not seen manifest, even though you have prayed? Does it appear that a cycle of failure has been established in your life? Are you seeing more promises not answered than you are seeing answered?

"'I know the plans that I have for you.' This message is from the Lord. 'I have good plans for you. I don't plan to hurt you. I plan to give you hope and a good future'" (Jeremiah 29:11 ERV). God's plan for us is good. He has designed a hope, the thing you live for, and a good future for you. What have you been hoping for? What prayer has been in your heart and on your lips daily? Do not continue to settle for less than what God has planned for you. The good future that God has designed for you includes His assistance in getting you there. Jeremiah needed God's assurance that He would help him. In Jeremiah 1:8, God told Jeremiah not to be afraid of their faces. Jeremiah was a young prophet in Israel. To prepare him for his assignment to speak the word of the Lord to the nation of Israel, God cautioned him not to be afraid. The leaders of Israel were not receptive to the Lord's message and neither were the citizens of Israel. The faces of the nation were against God and His prophets, but God assured Jeremiah that divine help would be made available to help him fulfill his call.

Similar promises are written throughout Scripture. God has made divine assistance available to you to fulfill your destiny. You might ask, "If God has planned this good future for me, why is my life not reflecting that good future?" The answer is simple. Just as God has determined a destiny for you, the enemy is equally determined to keep you from that good future. The kingdom of darkness plans traps, digs pits, lays snares and releases vexations and frustrations against you to prevent you from living out the good future and hope God has designed for you. Two life scripts have been written for you: One plan emanates from the Kingdom of God and the other from the kingdom of darkness. You will encounter resistance from the forces of darkness as you move forward into God's purpose for your life. Do not let the resistance stop you! God sends help from His sanctuary, bringing supernatural breakthrough as you develop the practice of strong, militant prayer. As you engage in this realm of prayer, you start to experience the awakening of every spiritual gift and promise in your life.

Strong, militant prayer binds the enemy's operations against you and initiates a release of everything that has been stolen and requires that it be returned with compensation. That is retribution!

Understanding Retribution

Retribution is payback. It is retaliation or punishment inflicted on someone as vengeance for a wrong or criminal act. Any time hell launches a plan against you, it is a criminal act, and it is important that you begin to regard delays, captured promises and other assignments of hell against you as criminal acts. Delays are attempts to capture the portion that God has for you. If you do not regard these events as criminal, you will think of them as just part of life on earth, and this holds you back from moving in violent prayer and faith that demands recovery of your goods.

What this means is that you can recover everything the enemy has stolen from you. What portion of your inheritance has been lost? What remains to be restored? If the enemy is attempting to steal your portion, he must repay more than what was taken. "A hungry man might steal to fill his stomach. If he is caught, he must pay seven times more than he stole" (Proverbs 6:30–31 ERV).

| LAW OF RETRIBUTION |

All believers have Kingdom authority to command the release of their captured goods with interest paid on what was stolen.

Hell is not entitled to your inheritance. A thief is required to repay up to seven times what was taken. You are entitled to the return of what was stolen, with interest on your stolen goods.

That is retribution. The problem with most believers is that they are unaware of the thief at work in their lives.

In Matthew 13:24, Jesus shares about a sower who sowed in his field, expecting a harvest. While the man slept, his enemy came and sowed tares among the wheat. This is how the enemy operates. While we sleep, hell is awake, implementing demonic assignments to stop us. How many times have you attempted to move your life forward, grow your ministry, grow your business, etc., and the opposite happens? Too many Christians are living in spiritual compromise, which creates spiritual dullness, and they are not even aware that a thief is operating against them. They just continue to go along with the status quo. This book is intended to awaken you to the truth, so you are able to see your prayers answered. It is possible for you to live your destiny and accomplish God's will for your life. Generational iniquities will be broken off your life, even though they may have plagued your bloodline for generations. The key is knowing how to pray until retribution manifests.

"From the days of John the Baptist until now the kingdom of heaven suffers violence, and the violent take it by force" (Matthew 11:12 NKJV). I am not using this verse to justify physical acts of violence. I am suggesting there is a dimension of prayer that believers can engage in wherein retribution is released on their behalf. Retribution is a war principle. The violence of the Kingdom of God is understanding how to partner with heaven, engaging in violent spiritual warfare that not only enforces the victories won at Calvary but forces the enemy to release your portion.

The Darkness of Ignorance

Too often we pray and wait, pray and wait, and we continue to pray and wait—but we never see the promises of God manifest.

We are not aware of the reason our prayers are not being answered, and we become frustrated and stop praying. Most of us assume that it is either not God's will or it is not God's time.

We are commanded not to be ignorant of spiritual things: "To keep Satan from taking advantage of us; for we are not ignorant of his schemes" (2 Corinthians 2:11 AMP). Satan looks for ways to take advantage of believers, and one of the primary ways he does this is through the spirit of ignorance. Releasing the spirit of ignorance is one of his most successful strategies.

I have stated often that the level of spiritual ignorance is too high among believers. We spend too little time in prayer and study of God's Word, which creates a deficiency of knowledge in our lives. More time is spent engaging in entertainments like television, movies, sporting events, social media, etc., and not enough time attending to spiritual matters. While these activities are not necessarily wrong, we must be certain that we spend adequate time engaging in the things of the Spirit of God to be able to live a balanced life. A life of entertainment with no spiritual development is not properly balanced, just as all spiritual development and nothing else is an improper balance. Ignorance causes us more suffering in life. When we decide to deal with spiritual ignorance, we are empowered to overcome every problem in life.

I started my career as an educator of young children, operating a successful early-education program. Within the first three years, I recognized that my level of knowledge in the area of child development was not as high as necessary. My desire was to serve young children in the best possible way, and I understood that a vital key in the educational success of young children was a quality preschool experience. If I was to accomplish my goal, it was imperative that I address my own lack of knowledge in the area of child development. I became determined to acquire the education I needed. This pursuit resulted in my earning three degrees in education over an eight-year period, an effort that required a tremendous amount of commitment and sacrifice. The point at which you start to overcome the mountain of lack of spiritual knowledge in your life is the moment when you are able to deal with problems that arise. Your dissatisfaction becomes the catalyst to a deeper pursuit.

What I did not know was that God would even use difficulties in my childhood to propel me forward. When I was a young girl, our home experienced seasons of chaos due to my stepfather, who was a functional alcoholic. There were days when the tenor of the house was loud and angry. My hiding place was books. My desire to read increased throughout my youth and early teenage years. I did not know then how the desire to read would help me build a strong foundation in the Word of God as a new believer. Not only that, my hunger for reading and knowledge would provide the foundation necessary to endure eight years in a university at a stage in life that made me a nontraditional student, meaning I was not around twenty years old.

When I purposed to gain knowledge in the area of child development, the early-education program I founded and operated grew into a successful elementary school, serving more than 150 students from kindergarten through eighth grade. I experienced harvest and business success because I was no longer operating in ignorance. Knowledge empowers you to lay hold of your inheritance—that is, your possessions. The Word of God exhorts us to apply ourselves to knowledge and understanding: "Apply your heart to understanding [seeking it conscientiously and striving for it eagerly]" (Proverbs 2:2 AMP). Proverbs also says, "Apply your heart to discipline and your ears to words of knowledge" (Proverbs 23:12 AMP).

Satan cannot contain believers who become knowledgeable about their spiritual rights and inheritance. When you are armed with knowledge, you are positioned to walk in dominion in every area of your life. Those who choose to remain spiritually ignorant will not experience the full measure of breakthrough in their lives that God has planned for them. Overcoming spiritual ignorance gives us the power to reign effectively as kings and priests on earth. This is the point at which we begin to experience responses to prayers and fulfillment of our dreams. Overcoming spiritual ignorance will position you to begin walking in dominion in every area of your life.

Spiritual ignorance is a condition that believers can no longer tolerate. Too much is at stake! Remaining under the cloak of spiritual ignorance gives the powers of darkness triumph over citizens of the Kingdom. As a believer, I have developed and maintained a consistent practice of study in the Word of God. Knowing what God says about a matter helps me to be more confident that my request is within God's will for me. My King wants me to know His promises for my life as a Kingdom citizen, and He wants you to know, too.

APPLICATION

Spend time daily reading the Word of God concerning His promises to you in the areas you need to experience retribution. This practice will help you overcome ignorance of God's promises to you.

God has provided an avenue of justice for us, the citizens of His Kingdom, and it is retribution. God is, among many other things, lawgiver and righteous judge. When our inheritance is held in the second heaven, this is illegal. Our prayers act as an appeal to heaven's courts. I like how God is described in Isaiah 33:22–23 (ERV): "The LORD is our judge. He makes our laws. He is our king. He saves us. The LORD will give us our wealth." This is retribution.

Suppose you discovered a thief had gained access to your house and was coming each day to steal something from you. Would you be content in allowing him to steal from you without calling the police? Of course not. Why then do we allow the enemy to steal without responding? Engaging in warfare prayer must be our response. Partnering with God, who is our righteous judge, must be our response. That partnership begins in prayer, knowing that God has given us an inheritance. It begins in knowing that God is a good Father who daily loads us with benefits (see Psalm 68:19). David sang about the many benefits of God in Psalm 103. Every 24-hour cycle of your life, God preloads benefits for you.

At one point in my life I worked for a major insurance company. When I was hired, I was given an employee handbook. My employers discussed many areas in the handbook at orientation, but I was instructed to familiarize myself with it so I would know what my benefits were. Whenever something happened that was in conflict with the handbook, I could go to Human Resources and ask for justice. That is how warfare works. If you are ignorant of your benefits or unaware of the thief, Satan will not stop! Warfare prayer ensures that we receive all of the benefits God has for us. Praying and believing for retribution when something has been stolen is the level of engagement at which each believer must become skilled. Today, choose to overcome and begin experiencing answers to your prayers. It is time for you to experience retribution in every area of your life. What has been stolen or delayed in your life must be returned with increase!

||||||||||||||||||||||||||||||||||||||||||||||||||||||||||||||||||||||||||||||||||||||||||||||||||||

Key Scriptures: Jeremiah 29:11; Matthew 11:12

Key Points: Law of retribution: You have the right to retribution when your portion has been stolen by the enemy.

- You can develop capacity to engage in militant warfare prayer.
- God is our lawgiver and our righteous judge.

Reflection: God called Jeremiah as a prophet to the nation of Israel. What has He called you to do? How do you need to engage in prayer to gain a clearer understanding of God's purposes for your life?

_____

_____

_____

_____

CHAPTER TWO

Where Did That Come From?

For our struggle is not against flesh and blood [contending only with physical opponents], but against the rulers, against the powers, against the world forces of this [present] darkness, against the spiritual forces of wickedness in the heavenly (supernatural) places.

Ephesians 6:12 AMP

The apostle Paul, when writing to the church in Ephesus, explains the struggle believers are facing on earth. This struggle is a kind of wrestling, which is a contest in which each participant endeavors to throw the other down or off balance. The contest is decided when the victor is able to hold his opponent down, preventing him from moving. This meaning also reflects the Christian's struggle with the power of evil.[1] Sometimes victory over evil requires wrestling, but far too many Christians overlook the reality of the struggle between light and darkness. We approach the issue of faith and prayers thinking that we only need to ask and wait. This is a common misconception. Seeing responses to our prayers not only includes asking in faith but gaining revelation concerning—and dealing with—any hindrances to our prayers.

In his description of the struggle between believers and the powers of darkness, Paul was describing an ongoing resistance. The goal of hell and its evils is to delay responses to our prayers. We are each grappling or wrestling in the Spirit against assignments of hell targeting our destinies. These assignments not only war against you to control your destiny, they war to gain control over your portion. Each of us has been given a portion from God; this is our inheritance. As we walk in dominion in some area, we gain access to our portion as we exercise rulership in that area. Hell's agenda is to stop you from accessing and walking in your portion.

> APPLICATION
>
> Ask the Lord to let you see (in the spiritual realm) how the forces of hell are operating against you, covering your portion.

Demon Structures

Paul not only provides a description of our spiritual struggle against the powers of darkness, he gives us a glimpse of the way the kingdom of darkness is structured when he explained to the Ephesian believers that their wrestling was "against the rulers, against the powers, against the world forces of this [present] darkness, against the spiritual forces of wickedness in the heavenly (supernatural) places" (Ephesians 6:12 AMP). The powers of hell are structured in such a way as to maximize their efforts against believers. Paul was using military language to describe the reality of the spiritual contest that confronts every believer every day. He was describing spiritual warfare. This warfare takes place continually across the earth, on several different levels. In his book *Warfare Prayer*, C. Peter Wagner describes three levels of spiritual warfare: ground level, occult level and strategic level. Let's take a closer look at each of these.

Ground-Level Warfare

The term *ground-level warfare* is commonly used to describe personal deliverance ministry, the ministry of casting out devils.[2] Deliverance ministry is an important aspect of Kingdom living and has been since Jesus was practicing it. When the disciples returned from their mission trips, they rejoiced that the demons were subject to them (see Luke 10:17). Casting out demons is part of the overall ministry of deliverance.

Much has been written about the debate over whether or not a Christian can have a demon. I believe the issue is not *can* Christians have a demon; in many instances, Christians *do* have a demon. This is because prior to salvation through Christ, our sin nature controls us. This sin nature causes the flesh to become accustomed to certain ways of living and being. Habits are entrenched in the soul realm. The ministry of deliverance is not about the demons; it is about bringing spiritual victory and freedom to those who are in bondage. Deliverance is about setting the captives free, which is accomplished through ground-level spiritual warfare. In Mark 7:27, Jesus made it clear that believers are entitled to deliverance; it is the "children's bread." This does not mean that believers are not responsible for praying, fasting and studying the Word of God. It does mean, however, that the supernatural ministry of deliverance is available to each and every believer.

In her book *How to Cast Out Demons*, Doris Wagner writes,

After passing the temptation in the wilderness, Jesus began to weaken the kingdom of darkness by casting out demons and showing his disciples how to do the same. In Mark 16:17–18 He even states, "These signs will follow those who believe. In My name, they will cast out demons . . . they will lay hands on the sick and they will recover." That seems to include us today. We should be continually pushing back the kingdom of darkness by being obedient to these orders. This level of ministry is ground-level warfare and should be a common level of ministry for all believers.[3]

Deliverance is part of the supernatural ministry of all believers and a significant area of ministry in the Church, especially for new believers. As a new believer, I was fortunate to join a Pentecostal ministry that believed in fasting, prayer, baptism in the Holy Spirit with the evidence of tongues and deliverance. Corporate deliverance meetings were known as "casting-out services." Prior to these services, we would fast for several days in preparation for personal deliverance.

During this season, I learned that I did not have to wait for the monthly corporate deliverance service; I could and did include deliverance in my times of personal prayer at home. I carried considerable anger and bitterness and needed much deliverance. I did not want to be saved and angry or saved and bitter, so I sought the Lord continually for deliverance. I believe that this pattern in my early Christian walk was a significant contribution to my continuing in the Kingdom, living a life of freedom and victory.

I remember watching people hear about the type of church I belonged to, and an eerie expression would come over their faces. It was almost as though they did not know if they should continue our conversation or if they should run. That reaction was typical of many misconceptions about Pentecostals that were common at the time. Some of the biggest misconceptions were in the area of deliverance. Unfortunately, these misconceptions continue among those who believe that Christians do not need deliverance. Nothing could be further from the truth.

Life in the earth realm brings many frustrations, disappointments and traumas. During these times we can suffer wounds in the soul realm that require deliverance. Jesus described deliverance as the children's bread. This is merely an indication that believers suffer wounds that need to be healed. Sometimes we are confronted by generational iniquities like gambling, pornography, lust and other issues passed down through our bloodlines. Looking back, we are able to see how these things were problematic to our forefathers. While some Christians are delivered at the time of salvation, others find that these areas continue to plague them. Deliverance is the answer.

APPLICATION

Commit to building and maintaining a life of prayer and worship and to developing a habit of studying the Word of God so your mind is renewed each day.

It is important to understand that deliverance is only the beginning. You must build and maintain a life of prayer and worship and develop a habit of studying the Word of God so your mind is renewed each day. In other words, you must allow the Spirit of God to fill you each day. When you do not, the enemy comes back with reinforcements.

> Now when the unclean spirit has gone out of a man, it roams through waterless (dry, arid) places in search of rest, but it does not find it. Then it says, "I will return to my house from which I came." And when it arrives, it finds the place unoccupied, swept, and put in order. Then it goes and brings with it seven other spirits more wicked than itself, and they go in and make their home there. And the last condition of that man becomes worse than the first.
>
> Matthew 12:43–45 AMP

As an apostle in a ministry, I have found that new believers are more successful living Kingdom lives when they have access to deliverance. Let's say a new believer has a demonic spirit of anger that manifests through his quick temper. A way to overcome this is through personal deliverance. The apostle Paul exhorted the Colossian church to put off "anger, wrath, malice, blasphemy, filthy language out of your mouth" (Colossians 3:8 NKJV). We are also instructed, "Do not hasten in your spirit to be angry, for anger rests in the bosom of fools" (Ecclesiastes 7:9 NKJV). Paul was speaking to believers in the Church who had not overcome these behaviors. Therefore, corporate and individual deliverance must be available to believers.

We need to understand ground-level warfare if we are going to experience a greater manifestation of answers to prayers. It is critical for us to recognize that the kingdom of darkness works against believers on a personal level.

Occult-Level Warfare

The occult promotes good works as a means of attaining salvation. Individuals under its influence promote an outward observance of spiritual things without redemption through the blood of Jesus and transformation by the Holy Spirit. This is another way that the kingdom of darkness withstands mankind to prevent us from moving in Kingdom truths. Occult-level warfare exposes the organized forces of darkness behind the occult, such as witchcraft, shamanism, Satanism, Freemasonry, Eastern religions, New Age and similar religious practices.

Interest in the occult is growing in Western society. We see this in the rising popularity of movies and television series such as the Harry Potter movies, *Charmed*, *Lucifer* and *Supernatural*. These are centered in the practice of magic, and many children and adults enjoy watching these programs. Wicca, a

34

contemporary form of witchcraft whose practice is usually hidden by its adherents, is also growing. According to the *New York Times*,

> It is unclear how many Wiccans and other pagans there are. The 2001 American Religious Identification Survey by the City University of New York found that Wicca was the country's fastest-growing religion, with 134,000 adherents, compared with 8,000 in 1990. The actual number may be greater.[4]

We also see increasingly violent and sexually explicit materials bombarding society through movies, video games and television programs. In 2000 Doris Wagner wrote,

> With so much violence, skewed values, and improper sexual input bombarding the minds and eyes of society, it is no wonder that after a time Generation X has become callused and confused and they just don't know right from wrong. But worse yet, they have almost no concept of evil . . . this leaves them vulnerable to innocently inviting demons into their lives because they don't know any better.[5]

All of this has led to a rejection of biblical values in American society since the 1960s, and subsequently it has continued.

This rejection of biblical values is seen in the percentage of millennials (reported by the Barna Group) who no longer identify with the Church:

> Over half of Millennials with a Christian background (fifty-nine percent) have, at some point, dropped out of going to church after having gone regularly, and half have been significantly frustrated by their faith. Additionally, more than fifty percent of eighteen to twenty-nine-year olds with Christian backgrounds say they are less active in church compared to when they were fifteen.[6]

While the reasons associated with the exodus from the Church are varied, the adverse effect on many believers of the attack on biblical values must be considered. The apostle Paul described the nature of this attack to his son in the faith, Timothy: "Holding to a form of [outward] godliness (religion), although they have denied its power [for their conduct nullifies their claim of faith]" (2 Timothy 3:5 AMP).

Rather than embracing Kingdom values, far too many believers have been influenced to find another door. Jesus reveals Himself in Scripture as the good shepherd who leads His sheep. "Most assuredly, I say to you, he who does not enter the sheepfold by the door, but climbs up some other way, the same is a thief and a robber" (John 10:1 NKJV). Throughout the gospels, Jesus reveals Himself as the access point to the Father: "Jesus said to him, 'I am the way, the truth, and the life. No one comes to the Father except through Me'" (John 14:6 NKJV).

Strategic-Level Warfare

Strategic-level warfare is also referred to as territorial warfare. Ephesians 6:12 is packed with descriptions of the kingdom of darkness; it shows us that the kingdom of darkness operates through an organizational, hierarchical structure. This demonic network is committed to interfering in the affairs of mankind, hindering our prayers and holding entire regions in captivity. Let's take a closer look at the biblical terms that describe this structure; their definitions and Strong's numbers are listed in the following table.

Greek Word	Strong's Number	Meaning	Notes
archē	746	principality	first-place rulers, magistrates of demons
exousia	1849	power	

Greek Word	Strong's Number	Meaning	Notes
kosmokrator	2888	world ruler	refers to the lords of this world, princes of this age of darkness; the devil and his demons
skotos	4655	night darkness	to have darkened eyesight or blindness (i.e., ignorance)
ponēria	4189	wickedness	depravity, iniquity, evil purposes and desires
epouranios	2032	high places	established in the heavenly places

From these word studies, several things should be noticed—the first being the hierarchical structure that operates within the kingdom of darkness. At the top of this structure are principalities and powers, which are territorial spirits assigned to regions, cities and nations. Throughout the New Testament, several other words are used in conjunction with the terms in Ephesians 6:12 to denote supernatural beings: *dynameis* (powers), *archōntes* (rulers), *thronoi* (thrones), *kyriotētes* (lordships), and *stoicheia* (elemental spirits).[7] The terms *arche* and *dynameis* are used primarily by Paul to designate angelic beings, both good and evil, but more commonly refer to the realm of Satan. In Ephesians, where there are more references to principalities and powers than in any other epistle, they are regarded as evil and under the authority of the devil.[8]

The point here is that principalities and powers are ruling spirits whose will and commands must be obeyed by the demon spirits with less authority. These fallen angels are subject to Satan's rule. Believers are called to resist their influence by appropriating the power of God, for the compelling influence of these evil powers has been broken by the finished work of Christ. When Christ was exalted to the right hand of God, He was placed in a position of authority far above every conceivable evil angelic being (see Ephesians 1:20–21).[9]

The Holy Spirit will come upon you and you will be filled with power.

Acts 1:8 TPT

Now you understand that I have imparted to you all my authority to trample over his kingdom. You will trample upon every demon before you and overcome every power Satan possesses. Absolutely nothing will be able to harm you as you walk in this authority.

Luke 10:19 TPT

Believers have been given power and authority to enforce the victory won by Christ at Calvary. In so doing, we access the blessings God has purposed for us. We have a choice as to which power we will serve, Satan's or God's.

Because principalities are territorial spirits, they work through the cultures of the regions to which they are attached. Cultures, of course, vary significantly from region to region, leading to distinctions in cultural practices, socioeconomic status and identity, among other factors. I remember a conversation on social media about adding sugar to grits. In case you do not know, grits, a hot breakfast dish popularized in the southern United States, has grown in popularity throughout the country. This dish is made from ground corn and can be eaten several ways. The fuss on social media was whether the most appropriate seasonings were butter, salt and pepper, or butter and sugar. I am still not sure which side won the debate. This is an example of how even minor practices vary from region to region. I have spent considerable time traveling and noticing differences in people. In some regions, they are very friendly, greeting and smiling at strangers they pass on the street. In other places, they are cold and distant, rarely making eye contact and hardly ever saying a friendly "hello."

38

When we see from a spiritual perspective, we realize that many differences we observe from region to region can be attributed to various territorial spirits operating over them. Since we cannot see these spirits naturally unless God reveals them, we must look at how their presence manifests in each region: In one region it could be gambling; in another, sex trafficking or higher levels of drug addiction and violent crime. We might see a combination of crimes. This is not simply due to different locations on the map. Cultural distinctions can be attributed to spiritual principalities, powers and rulers that operate over different cities, regions and territories. We can think of this as spiritual "air traffic control."

Recently, I dreamed I was inside of what looked like a demonic outpost. Everyone was dressed in military uniform. I noticed that the leader was not just overweight, he was grotesquely overweight. He was giving commands to other demons who reported to him. As I looked at him, I wondered why he was so large. The Lord imparted an answer to my spirit: The leader was so large because he was consuming the inheritance of believers. This ruling spirit was able to consume what belonged to believers who had become discouraged over what appeared to be unanswered prayers. The kingdom of darkness seeks to frustrate our purposes by hindering our prayers through delay.

As I looked around in the dream, I saw what looked like a communication structure, which was a command center. Lesser spirits manned the phones, and reports were completed and passed along to other spirits so that everyone knew what was going on. Because believers are not taking their positions in prayer and standing in their positions in the Kingdom of God, this highly organized and efficient demonic infrastructure has the capacity to prevail over many believers. This is a picture of how the kingdom of darkness operates.

Locating the Source of the Problem

> Our struggle is not against flesh and blood [contending only with physical opponents], but against the rulers, against the powers, against the world forces of this [present] darkness, against the spiritual forces of wickedness in the heavenly (supernatural) places.
>
> Ephesians 6:12 AMP

Principalities, rulers, powers and spiritual wickedness operate in high places, which are, as I wrote before, heavenly places. But where are they located? To understand where these demonic hindrances dwell, it is important for us to understand how God structured the heavens.

First Heaven

The first heaven is commonly referred to as the atmospheric heaven and includes the air that we breathe and the area immediately surrounding earth. Science refers to this as the troposphere, which extends from the surface of the earth to approximately 6 miles above, and the stratosphere, which extends 25 miles beyond the troposphere. The realm of the first heaven is referred to in Genesis 1:20: "Let birds fly above the earth across the face of the firmament of the heavens" (NKJV). Jesus indicated in Matthew 6:26 that our heavenly father would provide for all our needs in the realm of the first heaven, as he did for the "birds of the air" who dwell in it. James also makes mention of the first heaven when he said, "He prayed again, and the heaven gave rain, and the earth produced its fruit" (James 5:18 NKJV). In another translation, the word *heaven* is referred to as "sky": "Elijah prayed that it would rain. And the rain came down from the sky, and the land grew crops again" (James 5:18 ERV).

40

Second Heaven

The second heaven is the solar system (i.e., outer space). It is thought of as the stellar heaven, the place where the sun, moon and stars dwell. This is where powers of darkness reside, between heaven where God dwells and earth where mankind dwells. The biblical account of Creation reveals how God formed the second heaven on the fourth day.

> God made two great lights: the greater light to rule the day, and the lesser light to rule the night. He made the stars also. God set them in the firmament of the heavens to give light on the earth, and to rule over the day and over the night, and to divide the light from the darkness.
>
> Genesis 1:16–18 NKJV

When speaking of future events, Jesus also referred to this realm: "Immediately after the tribulation of those days the sun will be darkened, and the moon will not give its light; the stars will fall from heaven, and the powers of the heavens will be shaken" (Matthew 24:29 NKJV). Scripture refers to both heaven and the highest heavens in Deuteronomy 10:14 (NKJV): "Indeed heaven and the highest heavens belong to the LORD your God, also the earth with all that is in it." This helps us to understand the existence of the highest heaven where God dwells and the celestial heavens. Scripture also refers to heavens of heavens, indicating the same distinction: "Praise Him, you heavens of heavens, and you waters above the heavens!" (Psalm 148:4 NKJV).

Third Heaven

The realm of heaven where God's throne is established is often referred to as the third heaven. In the Scriptures, this realm of heaven is called "the dwelling place of God."

The LORD set his throne up in heaven, and he rules over everything.

Psalm 103:19 ERV

I looked, and there before me was an open door in heaven. And I heard the same voice that spoke to me before. It was the voice that sounded like a trumpet. It said, "Come up here, and I will show you what must happen after this." Immediately the Spirit took control of me, and there in heaven was a throne with someone sitting on it.

Revelation 4:1–2 ERV

Heaven belongs to the LORD, but he gave the earth to people.

Psalm 115:16 ERV

Heaven is God's command center. God mobilizes angelic forces from His throne in heaven, and He has assigned earth to mankind to steward. Although we are able to ascend to heaven through the door of worship and prayer, our human bodies are assigned to the earth realm.

Then I saw Heaven open wide—and oh! a white horse and its Rider. The Rider, named Faithful and True, judges and makes war in pure righteousness. His eyes are a blaze of fire, on his head many crowns. He has a Name inscribed that's known only to himself. He is dressed in a robe soaked with blood, and he is addressed as "Word of God." The armies of Heaven, mounted on white horses and dressed in dazzling white linen, follow him.

Revelation 19:11–14 MESSAGE

Like the apostle John in the book of Revelation, the apostle Paul described a supernatural experience wherein he was taken to the third heaven. The third heaven is where God's throne and the activity of heaven are centered. It is God's command center, often referred to as His war room. Paul describes being "caught up" or "taken up" to the third heaven and not knowing whether he was in his body or not. John describes falling down as though he were dead. From these encounters we know that overwhelming glory emanates from the place where God's throne and presence are.

> I know a man in Christ who was taken up to the third heaven. This happened 14 years ago. I don't know if the man was in his body or out of his body, but God knows. And I know that this man was taken up to paradise. I don't know if he was in his body or away from his body, but he heard things that he is not able to explain. He heard things that no one is allowed to tell.
>
> 2 Corinthians 12:2–4 ERV

Paul describes his encounter in the third heaven during which he did not know whether he was in his body or not. He describes receiving revelation that he was not permitted to reveal. Similarly, John heard an utterance from the seven thunders and was told to seal the things the seven thunders uttered and not to write them (Revelation 10:4 KJV). When we encounter the third heaven, we encounter the place where God resides and all of the surrounding activity of worship. There is no demonic activity in the third heaven.

Second-Heaven Interference

Each realm of heaven, first, second and third, reflect different functions. As discussed, the first heaven is the immediate domain that we encounter in the form of night, day, rain, etc. The third heaven is where God our Father, Jesus our Redeemer, the Holy Spirit, His angelic messengers and citizens of heaven live. It is the center of worship and mobilization of heaven's forces on behalf of God. The second heaven is where demonic principalities, powers, rulers and spiritual wickedness in high places reside. This realm is where demonic rulers and principalities operate to hinder the plans and purposes of God. It is here that responses to our prayers are often delayed.

Satan attempts to frustrate us by delaying answers to our prayers and, in some cases, deceiving us into believing that God has not responded. I want you to know that God always responds to our prayers. God's responses are yes, no or not yet. Do not be deceived into believing that God, our heavenly Father, the supreme ruler of the universe, is ignoring you. That is a lie of Satan. Not only is God not ignoring you, God has the capacity to do what you are asking of Him.

God is omnipotent, meaning He has all power. There is no power on earth or in the heavens that is stronger than God. The name El Gibhor in Jeremiah 32:18 reveals God as almighty! God cannot increase in might because He possesses all might.

God is omniscient, meaning God is all-knowing and cannot increase in knowledge. God is also omnipresent, meaning He is everywhere at the same time. In the psalms, David acknowledges that no matter where he goes, God is there with him, and God is with you.

> Where can I go from Your Spirit? Or where can I flee from Your presence? If I ascend to heaven, You are there; if I make my bed in Sheol (the nether world, the place of the dead), behold, You are there. If I take the wings of the dawn, if I dwell in the remotest part of the sea, even there Your hand will lead me, and Your right hand will take hold of me.
>
> Psalm 139:7–10 AMP

Finally, God is immutable, meaning He does not change. God is the same yesterday, today and forever. "For I am the LORD, I change not," He said (Malachi 3:6). And, "Jesus Christ is the same yesterday, and today, and for ever" (Hebrews 13:8).

God's will for you was planned in eternity before you were born. God knew who you would be, where you would live and what you would look like. He established your purpose, identity and destiny before you were born. As a matter of fact, God purposed that you would be sent to earth with His purposes in mind, to perform His will and to advance His Kingdom. God knows every thought of your mind and desire of your heart. Satan does not possess these characteristics. He would like us to think of him as a supreme being, but he is not. He is a fallen angel, who was cast out of heaven.

> How art thou fallen from heaven, O Lucifer, son of the morning! how art thou cut down to the ground, which didst weaken the nations! For thou hast said in thine heart, I will ascend into heaven, I will exalt my throne above the stars of God: I will sit also upon the mount of the congregation, in the sides of the north: I will ascend above the heights of the clouds; I will be like the most High. Yet thou shalt be brought down to hell, to the sides of the pit. They that see thee shall narrowly look upon thee, and consider thee, saying, Is this the man that made the earth to tremble, that did shake kingdoms?
>
> Isaiah 14:12–16 KJV

The enemy's efforts to delay our prayers is a carefully orchestrated attack against us. If you continue to bombard heaven with your requests, breakthrough will come. Responses will come from heaven. Delayed does not necessarily mean denied.

APPLICATION

Ask the Lord to let you "see" how the forces of hell are operating against you, covering your portion.

Key Scripture: Ephesians 6:12

Key Points: There are three realms of heaven:

- The first heaven refers to the atmospheric heaven and includes the air we breathe, the surface of the earth and the area directly above.
- The second heaven refers to outer space, where we find the solar system. This is where powers of darkness reside, the place between heaven where God dwells and earth where mankind dwells.
- The third heaven is where God dwells. In this realm, the throne of God is established.

Reflection: Have you sensed resistance in any area of your life or family? Ask the Lord to show you how demonic structures are operating against you or your family.

CHAPTER THREE

Interfering Forces

So he said to me, "O Daniel, you highly regarded and greatly beloved man, understand the words that I am about to say to you and stand upright, for I have now been sent to you." And while he was saying this word to me, I stood up trembling. Then he said to me, "Do not be afraid, Daniel, for from the first day that you set your heart on understanding this and on humbling yourself before your God, your words were heard, and I have come in response to your words. But the prince of the kingdom of Persia was standing in opposition to me for twenty-one days. Then, behold, Michael, one of the chief [of the celestial] princes, came to help me, for I had been left there with the kings of Persia. Now I have come to make you understand what will happen to your people in the latter days, for the vision is in regard to the days yet to come."

Daniel 10:11–14 AMP

What is happening when our prayers do not seem to be answered? When we experience delayed responses to prayer, we believe God desires to manifest certain promises over our lives, yet we do not experience the manifestation. When we do not see manifested responses to prayer, most of us assume that either the prayer was outside of God's will or it was not time for the manifestation of God's answer. We are assuming that we misunderstood what we heard God say in prayer or we misunderstood the prophecies spoken over our lives. At times, though, we are certain that the request is in agreement with the Word and God's will. While it is a legitimate possibility that our prayers were not in God's will, this is not always the case. Daniel shows us another possible reason for delayed responses to prayer.

When Daniel first began to pray, he experienced a 21-day delay in a response. Even though he had not received a response, however, Daniel responded correctly. Rather than becoming discouraged or assuming that God's answer was no, Daniel continued to engage in prayer for the full 21 days. In Daniel 10:11–14, his answer came in the form of an angelic visitation. He had been praying and waiting three straight weeks by that time. What was the problem? Why did 21 days have to elapse before Daniel received a response to his prayers?

The same Scripture gives the reason for the delayed response, when the angel declared that God had heard Daniel's prayers the very day he made his request. "Do not be afraid, Daniel, for from the first day that you set your heart on understanding this and on humbling yourself before your God, your words were heard, and I have come in response to your words" (Daniel 10:12 AMP).

Since Daniel's prayers were heard on the first day that he prayed, there must be another explanation for the delay besides that Daniel's prayer was outside of God's will. The purpose of this book is to provide insight into the spiritual roadblocks operating from the second heaven that prevent or hinder answers to prayer that are coming from God's throne. The kingdom of darkness strategically places these roadblocks to frustrate believers in their pursuit of answers to prayer. When this happens consistently, prayer becomes a burden rather than a joy. Hell does everything possible to discourage believers from receiving the responses they seek. Several things happen to us when our prayers are consistently unanswered:

1. Discouragement causes us to stop praying, resulting in insufficient communication between God and us.
2. Insufficient communication with God adversely affects our spiritual lives. Since prayer is a life source to the believer, the lack of prayer means that we will become spiritually deficient.
3. Prayer not only energizes our spiritual lives, but we enjoy phenomenal communication with God. We were created to hear the voice of God, and the lack of prayer results in our not accurately hearing God at the frequency on which He speaks.
4. We lack the necessary revelation for victory. Prayer releases tremendous revelation concerning events in our lives and on earth. During prayer, we are in position to hear what the Spirit of God is saying to the Church. This is called revelation. Prayer is not one-way communication; God continues to speak during our times of prayer.

APPLICATION

What have you been praying for that remains unanswered? Make a list and spend prayer time listening for God's response. God responds to our prayers.

During seasons of delayed responses, hell will try to influence you to believe that God does not care or that He will not respond. It is the goal of hell to influence believers to think that God is not involved in our everyday lives, though nothing could be further from the truth. We see this strategy in the Garden of Eden, where the serpent asked Eve, "Did God really tell you that you must not eat from any tree in the garden?" (Genesis 3:1 ERV). Satan always attempts to confuse you about God's intent for you. This is why we must be committed to daily prayer and study of the Word of God so that we are armed with the truth of God's intentions and desires for us. That is what revelation is: the light of God coming into an area of our minds where there is darkness, and we do not know what to do, or we need a strategy to move us forward. Revelation comes as light, showing us the way forward.

Assignments of Fear

Some years ago, one of my friends received her driver's license. As a new driver she was apprehensive about her new responsibility. One evening, as she was driving, she saw a tree and began saying to herself, "I am going to hit that tree!" She was overwhelmed by fear and could not stop looking at the tree. Within moments she had swerved off the street and hit the tree.

This is a perfect example of how fear operates. In Job 3:25, Job stated, "For the thing which I greatly feared is come upon me, and that which I was afraid of is come unto me." Fear is one of the first attacks of the enemy against us when we are experiencing delayed responses. In this case, the word *fear* implies that Satan means to frighten us. Daniel is told to not be frightened. What was he encouraged not to be frightened of?

Daniel was in a season of divine visitation. When heaven reveals itself to us in new ways, our first instinct is fear. In the book of Revelation, John encountered heaven and fell on the ground as though he were dead (see Revelation 1:17). As human beings, we are so tuned in to the frequency of earth that when we encounter heaven, a radically different atmosphere, we may draw back in fear. We become frightened.

The anxiety that accompanies fear creates chaos in our lives and impacts those around us. It stifles our thoughts, leads to destructive habits, and steals our peace.[1] No matter what you are afraid of, you need to remember that God will never reject you. The Lord wants to meet all of your needs. God tells us that He feeds the birds of the air and clothes the grass with the splendor of Solomon (see Matthew 6:25–30). Since God is carefully providing for creation, how much more will God respond to our prayers? We are made in the image and likeness of God, and His desire is to answer our prayers. Do not let fear drive you from the place of faith, just as Daniel did not. When the angel told Daniel to not be afraid, it was not only encouragement to gather his emotions so that he would understand heaven's response. The angel was also announcing that Daniel's season of waiting for a response had ended. No matter how long you have waited for heaven's response to your prayers, it is important to remember that God answers. He is a good Father, present in the lives of His children, and He always responds when we ask Him for something. Keep in mind that the answer might be yes, no or not yet—but God always responds.

APPLICATION

Are there areas of your life where fear is attempting to overcome you? Make a list of these areas, submit them unto the Lord and receive His peace.

We Need God's Anointing

Daniel 10:2–3 explains Daniel's attitude during the time of waiting. He was sad for three weeks; he changed his diet and anointed himself. When we are waiting for God's response, we must learn to pull aside from our daily habits as much as possible and anoint ourselves during the wait. Anointing represents the overflow of God. It is the fatness, the abundance of God upon our lives. "So it will be in that day, that his burden will be removed from your shoulders and his yoke from your neck, and the yoke will be broken because of fatness" (Isaiah 10:27 NASB). When the enemy attempts to place his yoke upon us, Scripture declares that the yoke will be destroyed. The yoke is shattered because of the bull's fat, a type of God's anointing. The burdens are destroyed!

During Isaiah's time, oxen were beasts of burden. When they had an abundance of grass to eat, they became fat. As they grew fatter and fatter, the yokes on their backs carrying the burdens would break. From a practical point of view, when we are smeared with an abundance of God's anointing, our burdens are destroyed. This means the enemy's efforts to withhold from us what God has promised are defeated. Any unrighteous edicts spoken against us by hell cannot stand when God has spoken.

The overflow of God's anointing is necessary. The measure of the anointing that you walked in this past season was good for that season. You need a new measure for the present season. Each new season brings with it a new season of warfare. Your assigned purposes and destiny are assaulted by hell with greater intensity. Jesus encountered the enemy during His forty days in the wilderness. He encountered hell in a more significant way when He was on His way to Calvary. Jesus carried the power of the anointing upon His life in every circumstance. It was a natural part of His daily life, including healing the sick, raising the dead, casting out devils—even when it was time to go to the cross. Right now, let a fresh anointing be released over you as you pray this prayer:

Lord, I thank You for the anointing. Right now, I receive a fresh anointing, fresh oil, upon my life. As I spend time in prayer, worship and the study of Your Word, I am growing fatter. As I grow fatter, every yoke the enemy has tried to place upon me breaks off now, in Jesus' name. You are increasing me more and more. I take on the yoke of the Lord, for Your yoke is easy and Your burden is light. Let the anointing to excel and prosper be released upon every area of my life beginning today, in Jesus' name.

| LAW OF THE ANOINTING |

When the anointing increases in the life of a believer, every demonic yoke that hell has tried to place upon him or her must break.

Anointing represents being "smeared" with purpose. As a believer, you have been anointed for God's plans. This means that God has set you aside and consecrated you for His purposes. The Old Testament priests were anointed prior to serving in the Temple. Their right ears, right thumbs and right big toes were anointed with ram's blood, and then their garments were sprinkled with ram's blood and specially prepared oils (see Exodus 29:20–21). This anointing signified that their hearing, strength and direction in life were dedicated to God's purposes. When you are waiting for God's promises to manifest, for responses to your prayers, you must receive God's anointing. Without the anointing, we become tired and discouraged; many leave the place of prayer without seeing a full manifestation of God's promises for them, because they did not have sufficient anointing to wait.

The anointing is not just a benefit of following God; it is something we need. As Benny Hinn explains,[2] its effects on our lives are far reaching. Among them:

1. God's anointing will change your life as revelation flows into you, bringing light and illumination and showing you the path ahead.

2. God's anointing brings provision. The widow in 1 Kings 17 received an increase of oil, which represents the anointing. Her willingness to sow a seed into the life of the prophet Elijah opened heaven's doors to release increase upon her; that increase would take her through a season when everyone around her was experiencing drought and lack, but she and her son experienced abundance.

3. God's anointing brings blessings. Psalm 133 speaks of the commanded blessing that flowed from the beard of Aaron. Scripture also tells us that all of God's promises are yes and amen (see 2 Corinthians 1:20). God's anointing brings blessings upon our lives.

God's anointing breaks the enemy's yokes. Satan's yokes lay on us oppressions and burdens that hold us back from God's purposes. When you are in the season of waiting for answers to your prayers to manifest, an anointing for patience helps you to endure and stand in faith. When we become yoked with unbelief, the place of prayer leaves us discouraged rather than encouraged. Do not confuse waiting with idleness. In the waiting, we learn to hear God's voice in a clear way. We learn to listen for strategies that move us toward manifestations of His promises.

One of the most difficult times to endure is the season of waiting. Waiting is difficult! This is why we need patience, one of the fruits of the Spirit, to be developed in us. This happens during times of waiting. In these seasons, divine instructions enable us to overcome any interference from the second heaven that might be holding our blessings. Without God's anointing, we can become overeager and move forward in human wisdom and not God's wisdom. When we receive a fresh anointing for the wait, we begin to hear clear direction from God concerning

His plan and purpose in the situation. God is not inconsistent in His dealings with us. All that God does is intertwined and interconnected, bringing us into His best plans. A fresh anointing is necessary to perceive His voice and hear His plans. Without God's anointing, fear overtakes us and moves us away from God's intended pathway.

The Scriptures declare that the yoke will be destroyed. "So it will be in that day, that the burden of the Assyrian will be removed from your shoulders and his yoke from your neck. The yoke will be broken because of the fat" (Isaiah 10:27 AMP). The yoke is shattered because of the bull's fat, a type of God's anointing. The burdens are destroyed!

This means that any effort of the enemy to withhold from us what God has promised is defeated. Any unrighteous edicts spoken against us by hell cannot stand when God has spoken. Right now, let a fresh anointing be released over you as you pray this prayer.

> *Heavenly Father, I receive the anointing that I need to wait for the manifestation of the answers to my prayers. I will not get ahead of You. Right now, I choose Your way over my way. My ears are open to hear Your strategies that will result in the full release of all that You have promised me concerning this issue. Show me how to pray, how to worship and how to war for the release of what You have promised me. Amen.*

Overcome Fear

As we wait with patience on the promises of God, we have to be prepared to battle fear. And we must regard it as an enemy, for fear is an interfering force that comes against our lives. It is not God's desire for us. As the angel said to Daniel, "Do not

55

be afraid, Daniel, for from the first day that you set your heart on understanding this and on humbling yourself before your God, your words were heard, and I have come in response to your words" (Daniel 10:12 AMP). Throughout Scripture, God commands us to not fear. Instead we are to take courage in the fact that God is more than able to overcome our enemies, bring us through difficult circumstances and establish us in His promises. Fear positions us in unbelief, which is the opposite of faith. Fear implies that God cannot or will not do what He has promised.

> Fear thou not, for I am with thee; be not dismayed, for I am thy God. I will strengthen thee; yea, I will help thee; yea, I will uphold thee with the right hand of My righteousness. Behold, all they that were incensed against thee shall be ashamed and confounded; they shall be as nothing, and they that strive with thee shall perish. Thou shalt seek them and shalt not find them, even them that contended with thee. They that war against thee shall be as nothing, and as a thing of naught. For I, the LORD thy God, will hold thy right hand, saying unto thee, "Fear not; I will help thee."
>
> Isaiah 41:10–13

When we operate from a position of fear, we cannot overcome any obstacles, so we are not able to see more responses to our prayers. Under fear's influence, we question God's intention and ability to respond to our requests. We wonder if God will answer or if our prayers are in God's will. How many times have we left the place of prayer before seeing God's response? I believe when we transition into eternity to be with Jesus, we will become aware of the times we were on the threshold of breakthrough, of seeing a response to our prayers, and became discouraged one day before or one week before the response came.

| LAW OF FEAR |

When we operate from a position of fear, we cannot overcome the demonic obstacles hindering our prayers.

Although Daniel waited 21 days before he received a response, I believe that he was prepared to wait as long as it took. This kind of determination has what I like to call a "long-distance anointing." It is a sign that we have allowed the Spirit of God to develop a waiting attitude within us. By releasing an anointing to wait, this waiting attitude helps us overcome fear. God promises to strengthen us as we wait.

> But those who wait for the LORD [who expect, look for, and hope in Him] will gain new strength and renew their power; they will lift up their wings [and rise up close to God] like eagles [rising toward the sun]; they will run and not become weary, they will walk and not grow tired.
>
> Isaiah 40:31 AMP

He upholds us with His righteous right hand. This means that we cannot fall—God is holding us up! We are not standing in our own strength. We are standing in the strength of the Lord, who helps us. When hell has enlarged its mouth over us, taunting us, God helps us. Those who taunted you, every demon from hell that stood against you, will bow and submit to God's will, releasing every blessing that is being held back in the second heaven, because God is with you, helping you.

The Power of Your Words

The angel announced that he had come because of Daniel's words. The words we utter in prayer are heard at the throne of God, and God's responses are delivered by His angels. In

Daniel's case, the angel had been dispatched with a response on the first day that Daniel had prayed, though he had been hindered by the prince of the kingdom of Persia. Daniel's prayer had been answered on the first day that he set his mind to wait before God in fasting and humility.

Daniel did not complain at the apparent delay; he waited in prayer. Heaven's response had already been released by Daniel's words. Too often we underestimate the power of our words—though we are made in the image and likeness of God, possessing creative ability, we often overlook it. Our words have creative power, and every time we speak, we are creating something. When we speak words aligned with God's Word, both His written Word and His prophetically received words, we are creating. Faith-filled words bring us into agreement with what God has already spoken concerning the issue, and as citizens of the Kingdom of God, we are enforcing the judgments of God against our enemies. The Bible commands us to speak to insurmountable situations.

> Jesus was matter-of-fact: "Embrace this God-life. Really embrace it, and nothing will be too much for you. This mountain, for instance: Just say, 'Go jump in the lake'—no shuffling or shilly-shallying—and it's as good as done. That's why I urge you to pray for absolutely everything, ranging from small to large. Include everything as you embrace this God-life, and you'll get God's everything."
>
> Mark 11:22–24 MESSAGE

Our words are creatively powerful. Everything within earth's realm has been put under subjection to us. When we speak God's Word, everything must align with our words. Jesus was not only our Redeemer, He was an educator, a trainer of leaders. As He walked with the Twelve, He demonstrated the power of words. Finding a fig tree that did not produce fruit, Jesus said to the tree, "People will never eat fruit from you again" (Mark 11:14 ERV). The next day, the disciples noticed that the fig tree was dry and dead. Jesus explained to His followers the principle of creative power.

At a conference I attended, Dr. Caroline Leaf taught, "We are always in a Genesis moment. When we speak, we are creating and bringing forth in the earth. We are either creating heaven or creating hell." Everything God created has the capacity to hear. Jesus demonstrated the law of language creativity: You will have what you say. It is critical that you understand how powerful you are. Just by speaking, you can create! This means not only does the first heaven respond to you, but the second heaven must also respond to you. When you speak words filled with fear and unbelief, you release hell's interfering forces to operate against you. Commit today to agreeing with heaven.

LAW OF LANGUAGE CREATIVITY

You will have what you say.

This is what dominion looks like. God put everything in creation under the rulership of Adam and Eve. The law of dominion continues today.

LAW OF DOMINION

God gave mankind dominion; therefore, everything in the created order is subject to human beings.

You are an intricate part of God's plan. You have the capacity to rule. Our primary key of rulership is through the words we speak, creating something every time we speak. When you know that you have prayed according to God's will, you must continue standing on God's word, commanding that everything else bow! Satan is depending on your ignorance in this area.

Resistance Is Not Futile

I have been a fan of *Star Trek* over the years. The stated mission for the series is simple: "To boldly go where no man has gone before," a mission that remained the same through several iterations of the series. In *Star Trek: The Next Generation*, the starship *Enterprise* encounters an enemy called the Borg. Half-organic, half-machine, this enemy also has a sole mission: to assimilate all life forms into its collective. All life forms will be absorbed until one single form remains: Borg. In this form, no one would think or act independently. When the Borg encounter resistance, its declaration is, "Resistance is futile." The Borg's form and size are predicated on the stealing of other cultures.

This is how the enemy operates against us. The goal of hell is to assimilate you into the collective of those who no longer stand in faith, believing for the manifestation of their prayers. Hell taunts us the same way as the Borg: "Resistance is futile." No matter how much you resist, hell insists, you will never break through; you will never receive the full release of your inheritance.

Hell works to capture the portion assigned to us by taunting us with lies designed to frustrate us to the point of unbelief. When we are positioned in unbelief, we will not prevail over the enemy. We must continue to stand in faith, resisting the resistor, which is hell. Do not surrender your inheritance. Do not stop believing that God answers your prayers. Like Daniel, position yourself in prayer, fasting and worship. This must always be your response to hell. Do not let present warfare obscure God's promises. We overcome by faith, and faith comes through the Word of God. Not only will you receive your portion, but hell must give you more than what was originally stolen. That is retribution! It is supernatural payback for illegal operations in your life.

The only authority hell has over you is in what you surrender to it. Illegal delays are an attempt to steal what God has promised you. When this happens, you can demand not just your portion but interest on the return. It is time for you to take a stand against the enemy. Your resistance is not futile. Receive heaven's assistance to overcome the powers of hell that have come to steal your portion, frustrate your purpose and hinder your destiny. I encourage you to take a new stand today. It is time for you to experience retribution!

Just as the messenger angel came as a response to Daniel's words, the angels of the Lord will come in response to your words. Because Daniel purposed to fast and pray before the Lord, a response was dispatched to Daniel by the messenger angel. Hell's attempts to block the messenger were futile. The Bible names this interference the "prince of Persia." This territorial principality over the region was attempting to stop the communication to Daniel. When resistance manifested, God dispatched a warrior angel—one of the chief angels, Michael—to not only engage this demonic prince but to overcome him. You see, demonic attacks released from the second heaven and designed to illegally hold back blessings that belong to us are a reality. The principalities, powers, rulers of darkness and spiritual wickedness in high places form a demonic network designed to retain our blessings, attempting to prevent us from walking in the fullness of all that the Lord has for us by stealing part of our inheritance.

Daniel understood what to do in the season of waiting. He knew that humbling himself in prayer, fasting and worship would result in a response to his prayers. Daniel knew that God would respond, and that no matter what the cause of the delay, he would receive an answer. Like Daniel, purpose to wait before the Lord. Spend time in worship, prayer and fasting. As you partner with heaven, you will receive a response to your prayers, resulting in the defeat of interfering forces. Do not let fear overcome you. Posturing yourself in worship will fill you with anointing; your capacity will increase, and any yoke the enemy has tried to place upon you will be destroyed.

|||||||||||||||||||||||||||||||||||||||||||||||||||||||||||||||||||||||||||||||||||||||||||||||

Key Scriptures: Mark 11:23; Isaiah 41:10–13

Key Points:

- Law of fear: When you are positioned in fear, you cannot overcome the obstacles of hell that are hindering your prayers.
- Law of language creativity: You have what you say. God created creation by the power of His words. Mankind was created in the image and likeness of God. Whenever you speak, you are creating something.
- Law of dominion: God gave mankind dominion; therefore, everything in the created order is subject to human beings.

Reflection: How is the spirit of fear trying to gain an advantage over you? Review your conversations over the past few days. Do your words agree with God?

_____

_____

_____

_____

_____

_____

CHAPTER FOUR

Defeating Demonic Carpenters

"If anyone fiercely attacks you it will not be from Me. Whoever attacks you will fall because of you. Listen carefully, I have created the smith who blows on the fire of coals and who produces a weapon for its purpose; and I have created the destroyer to inflict ruin. No weapon that is formed against you will succeed; and every tongue that rises against you in judgment you will condemn. This [peace, righteousness, security, and triumph over opposition] is the heritage of the servants of the LORD, and this is their vindication from Me," says the LORD.

Isaiah 54:15–17 AMP

Dreams are one way God communicates with me. Not every dream I have is a message from God, but many are. Several years ago, I had a dream that looked like a typical scene from a war movie. I was being pursued by dark forces. In every house where I found refuge, my location became known to them, and they would then try to find a way in. Each time I escaped. Toward the end of the dream, I was walking across a lawn in front of a house, which I consider to be a type of threshold between the street and the entrance of the house. I had been hiding in a house, and as I exited, the dark forces started to engage me. I began to battle against them with everything I had. It seemed as though the battle had just begun when a voice from heaven suddenly spoke. "Safe passage!" I knew this was God's voice. In that moment, all of the dark forces froze in their tracks—no one moved. God spoke again, "Safe passage." I could see the sun rising in the distance, representing a new day, and I walked toward it.

What was God saying in this dream? I believe the interpretation is that no matter what dark forces come against you, God has the final word. God's word is absolute in all matters when He declares, "Safe passage!" Every dark force working against me had to cease. God tells Israel, "No weapon that is formed against you will succeed; and every tongue that rises against you in judgment *you* will condemn" (Isaiah 54:17 AMP, emphasis added). God has given you authority over your enemies, and *you* condemn every tongue!

Though our victory is sure, we still must recognize how Satan and his forces come against us so that we can confront them in the wisdom of the Lord. Among the forces he releases against us are demonic "carpenters." Demonic carpenters are dark forces that operate against you by trying to construct a different reality for you than the one God intends. These dark forces operate within a highly structured framework and have a singular focus: frustrating your purpose by hindering your prayers. The enemy believes if he can frustrate your purpose by hindering your prayers, you will become disillusioned and stop praying. When you stop praying, unbelief and discouragement takes the place of faith, and your heart begins to grow cold toward the Lord. Ephesians 6:12 admonishes us that we do not contend against flesh and blood. Your fight is not against your neighbor, co-worker or family member with whom you have an unresolved issue. Your fight is against demonic rulers committed to keeping you from seeing promises of God manifest in your life. God has given you spiritual weapons to fight and prevail against demonic powers. God has given you the weapon of prayer to overcome your enemy. Satan does not play fairly; he uses your weakness against you to overcome you. *But*, when you commit to prayer, God will give you strategies to overcome your enemy, and you will triumph. "But thanks be to God, who always leads us in triumph in Christ" (2 Corinthians 2:14 AMP).

Demonic forces operate in a type of confederacy, which is defined as a league or compact for mutual support or common action; it is an alliance of people or groups formed for an illicit purpose. Another way to look at this structure is to think of gangs or teams. I want you to notice how Satan not only mobilizes demonic forces against you, he also constructs demonic structures designed to entangle you, which will then hinder and frustrate you. Thus we see demonic carpenters operating in opposition to us, working to establish a demonic stronghold within us. This stronghold becomes a base of operation for the enemy.

Demonic confederacies sometimes operate through a local confederation of people. In his book *The Future War of the Church*, Chuck D. Pierce discusses Satan's confederation:

> Even though we are not warring against flesh and blood, the demonic forces in an area are usually working through a group of people who have aligned themselves with Satan through idolatrous worship, forming a churchlike entity—a fellowship devoted to Satan. Such confederations can take on many forms, including covens of witches, churches of Satan, Wicca groups and pagan worship.[1]

In many instances, Satan uses people to advance his agenda on earth. Perhaps you are being oppressed by an employer or co-worker. Maybe attacks are perpetrated against you by someone else you come in contact with. Is it possible that Satan is using these individuals to attack you and frustrate you as you move toward seeing God's promises released on your behalf through prayer? This is not an encouragement to become suspicious of everyone around you, but in some instances, this might be exactly what is happening. That is why you must operate in the gift of discernment, which is one of the spiritual weapons we will discuss in chapter 10.

Unforgiveness

Satan uses weapons such as demonic arrows to pierce your soul. These arrows can come in the form of hurtful words spoken to you by someone, disappointment, unresolved traumas from your childhood or betrayal in a relationship. When your soul is pierced with a demonic arrow, if the issue is unresolved, you can suffer a setback in seeing your prayers answered.

Let's consider the issue of unforgiveness. When you choose not to forgive, it is like dropping the anchor of your life into a moment in time when you were wounded by another. This anchor keeps you tied to your past. Demonic carpenters have free access to you, constructing walls around you to isolate you—not only from the people who hurt you but from positive relationships as well. Unforgiveness can lead to resentment, bitterness and mistrust, thereby separating you from others. It is possible that the people who offended you are unaware of what happened as a result of their actions. They may sense a change in your emotions without understanding that you are harboring unforgiveness. This change is directly related to your thought processes and behaviors. When this happens, you will not see the measure of response to prayer that you desire because you are harboring unforgiveness.

If you forgive others their trespasses [their reckless and willful sins], your heavenly Father will also forgive you. But if you do not forgive others [nurturing your hurt and anger with the result that it interferes with your relationship with God], then your Father will not forgive your trespasses.

Matthew 6:14–15 AMP

Peter raised the issue of forgiveness with Jesus in Matthew 18, asking Jesus how often he should forgive his brother. Peter probably knew the number seven was considered the number of completion and perfection. He was assuming that if he forgave seven times, this was all God required of him. But Jesus responded by telling Peter he was required to forgive seventy times seven, or nearly five hundred times. In other words, Jesus was telling Peter that he must be prepared to forgive every time someone transgressed against him. When we receive forgiveness from God, it is eternal. The reference to seventy times seven is representative of the eternal forgiveness that we extend to our transgressors. It seemed that Peter did not remember Jesus' earlier teaching on forgiveness.

Growing up in a home with a stepparent who was a functional alcoholic was not easy. Although I found a hiding place in books, at times I was affected by the angry noise that would often arise in our home. The effect on my life manifested in anger and resentfulness. I could not understand why our home was not like the homes of my friends. My perception was that their homes were quiet, and no family member spoke in anger to another. I thought their homes were always filled with laughter and kind words. This perception became the catalyst of overwhelming anger, and I developed resentment toward my parents that grew into unforgiveness and bitterness. I had been pierced with a demonic arrow of offense. The feelings remained with me until I surrendered my life to the Lord. As I surrendered my life to the Lord and received deliverance, the Holy Spirit began revealing the bitterness and unforgiveness in my heart. Although I wanted to be free, I just could not seem to overcome in this area. Thank God for His grace and mercy. What I could not surrender in my own strength, the Holy Spirit helped me to surrender. I began walking in total freedom.

When you are pierced by a demonic arrow, it can come in the form of offense or some other issue. It is important to recognize these circumstances as an attempt by Satan to pierce you. I often hear people say, "I will never forgive that person!" This is tragic simply because when we choose to hold on to the wrong that has been done to us, we are locked in that moment in time. Forgiveness is liberating. It is not easy to forgive someone who has wounded you. Maybe the offense against you was a horrific event that you have kept secret for many years. If you want to experience more answers to your prayers, you must allow Holy Spirit to help you to forgive. He helps us when we are weak. Those things that we cannot do in our own strength, Holy Spirit helps us. If you have dropped anchor on a situation in your life and have not been able to move forward, choose today to let it go. Forgiveness is a key to defeating demonic carpenters that might be operating in your life. Remember the words of Jesus: "If you are not willing to forgive, you won't be forgiven."

LAW OF FORGIVENESS

Forgive and you will be forgiven.

APPLICATION

Ask the Lord to show you anyone against whom you are harboring a spirit of unforgiveness. As Holy Spirit brings situations and people before you, surrender each situation to the Lord. Do not attempt to justify your feelings, just release them to the Lord.

It is time for you to move forward into your destiny. Do not choose to remain in a place of unforgiveness. A simple prayer for these times follows.

Today, I choose to forgive those who have offended and wounded me. I give up my right to be angry or carry thoughts of vengeance. Lord, vengeance belongs to You, and I place this issue in Your hands, trusting Your ways and not my own. I release myself from every demonic arrow the enemy has tried to pierce me with. Instead, I send the fiery arrow of the Lord to the camp of the enemy. I decree that the arrow the enemy has tried to pierce me with, he is pierced with himself. Today, I choose to meditate on the Word of God and not on the wrongs done to me. As I pray, everything concerning my potential that has died as a result of unforgiveness is being resurrected now. According to Isaiah 60:1–5, it is my time to rise and shine, for the Light of the Lord is rising upon me. Right now, every dormant gift within me is being resurrected. I pray this in the name of Jesus!

Familial Spirits

Releasing familial spirits to operate in our lives is another way demonic confederacies operate against you. This may also be referred to as generational iniquity. Familial spirits or generational iniquities are passed down from generation to generation. We can see this in families struggling with issues of domestic violence. Research shows that children who grew up in families marked by domestic violence often find themselves in similar situations as adults.[2] Drug addiction or alcoholism in the family often continues among children raised by alcoholic parents.[3] This is an iniquitous pattern, a manifestation of iniquity that has been passed down from generation to generation. Chuck Pierce discusses iniquitous patterns and familial spirits in *The Spiritual Warfare Handbook*:

> Through the sin and iniquitous pattern, a familial spirit controls a certain person in a family. Sin is an opening for demonic forces to work in subsequent generations of a family through the iniquity produced. They know the family weaknesses, and therefore entice, tempt, or lure family members with that weakness into the same or related sin. Spirits that are assigned to a family are called familial spirits. Some have been in families for generations on end.[4]

In this pattern of generational iniquities, resulting in familial spirits operating within a family, the enemy operates generationally. God manifests Himself as the God of Abraham, Isaac and Jacob. Satan, in counterfeiting whatever God does, also operates within a generational structure.

> Josiah was eight years old when he became king, and reigned for thirty-one years in Jerusalem. . . . He did what was right in the sight of the LORD and walked in all the ways of his father (ancestor) David, and did not turn aside to the right or to the left.
>
> 2 Kings 22:1–2 AMP

You can choose righteousness, regardless of the iniquitous patterns in your family line. Josiah looked back more than ten generations in his family line before finally choosing King David, a man after God's heart, as his example for living. The result of Josiah's decision was the reestablishment of a pattern of righteousness, which his grandfather Manasseh had chosen to ignore. You can follow Josiah's example. If there are iniquitous patterns in your bloodline like alcohol, drugs, pornography addiction or some similar issue, you can choose to walk in righteousness. If you are struggling with iniquitous patterns that have been passed down in your bloodline, you can be free today. This simple prayer will help move you toward freedom:

Father, I thank You for the power of redemption paid for me through the life, death, burial and resurrection of Jesus. Lord, thank You for revealing iniquitous patterns that are affecting me and hindering my prayers. These patterns are things that became part of my life as I grew up watching behaviors in my family. I acknowledge that these patterns are unrighteous and do not agree with Your Word. They hinder my prayers. Lord, I repent today and refuse to walk in ungodly patterns. Beginning today, let me walk in the redemptive gifts You have placed in my family. Like Josiah, I choose to walk in righteousness. Today, I choose freedom, in Jesus' name.

Thrones of Iniquity

Thrones of iniquity can operate in a region, providing Satan with access to entire regions. Thrones speak of government or rulership and can be established within families and regions. Demonic carpenters are working to build dark access points of control. Chuck Pierce explains that

Satan's objective is to block the plans of God by establishing his legal right to control an area. . . . Satan gains access in an area the same way he gains access to an individual's life or family line: through sin. He does this by encouraging individual or family sin to escalate into corporate sin. When corporate sin enters into our assigned boundaries, we need to be aware of how that sin can build a throne of iniquity and how we, being positioned in God's army, have the authority to dismantle it. Corporate sin—for example, idolatry, bloodshed, immorality and covenant breaking—creates a break in God's purpose, or order, for a region. Once this break begins to occur, Satan will take advantage to gain an upper hand and begin to establish his influence in that area. From that place of influence, Satan can build a throne upon which he is seated in a territory.[5]

Satan establishes himself as a counterfeit authority within a region, seeking to draw the entire region to his false light. Ultimately, Satan's desire is to establish himself within a region as the object of worship. This has been his singular goal, to exalt himself above God and become the object of man's worship. When this happens, God's authority is rejected. Pierce continues,

> Satan knows that men and women were created as vessels of worship and, whether they realize it or not, they will worship something. The simple fact is that either they are worshiping the true and living God or they are worshiping Satan and his demonic forces, whether overtly or through their sin (whether sins of omission or commission). It is this corporate sin that builds the foundation of the throne on which Satan is seated, and it is from that throne that demonic forces work to perpetuate the sin and establish the throne of iniquity to an even greater extent.[6]

Satan is always looking for an opportunity to control entire family lines, which then creates demonic access into regions. Prayer is a way to keep ourselves connected to God's Kingdom agenda, accessing Kingdom power and strength to overcome every assignment of the enemy against us. "The LORD has established His throne in the heavens, and His sovereignty rules over all [the universe]" (Psalm 103:19 AMP).

Prayerlessness, then, creates the opportunity for Satan to enter and entrench his agenda into our lives. Prayer is the key strategy helping us to resist the enemy's attacks. Developing skills to engage in the type of prayer that brings forth manifestations of

God's will and purpose in your life is vital. God is the supreme ruler of the universe. No matter how powerful Satan's kingdom *seems* to be, God rules over all! God's plan will be fulfilled on earth. It includes freedom and victory for you over every obstacle the enemy places on your path. No matter how long you have waited for the manifestation of God's promises, His plan will come to pass. As you partner with God and develop the strategies of violent prayer, demonic carpenters that are trying to hinder you will be defeated. This is God's will and desire for you.

Demonic Altars

Demonic altars are established in a family or territory through false worship. When God delivered Israel out of Egypt, the first thing He did was establish the pattern of worship. Generations of the children of Israel had grown up in Egypt worshiping idols according to the pattern in the kingdom of darkness. Now God was liberating His people with His mighty arm so they could learn how to worship Him, the supreme ruler of the universe. God's intent was for the Israelites to know Him through worship and reject the pattern of worship at demonic altars that they had learned in Egypt. This proved problematic for Israel, as they continued to return to false patterns of worship.

The book of Judges demonstrates a cycle of worship at demonic altars to which the people of Israel continually gave themselves over. Judges 6 describes a young man named Gideon, whose father, Joash, worshiped at the altar of Baal. As the patriarch of the family, Joash would have instructed Gideon in the family pattern of worship. No wonder Gideon responded in unbelief when the angel of the Lord spoke to him. Gideon had never heard Baal speak to him, and I am sure he was not expecting to hear God speak to him that day, either.

The angel of the LORD appeared to Gideon and said, "The LORD be with you, brave soldier." Then Gideon said, "Pardon me, sir, but if the LORD is with us, why are we having so many troubles? We heard that he did wonderful things for our ancestors. They tell us the LORD took them out of Egypt. But now it seems the LORD has left us and is letting the Midianites defeat us."

Judges 6:12–13 ERV

APPLICATION

Ask the Lord to show you any familial spirits or thrones of iniquity in your bloodline that might be operating against you.

Gideon recognized that God's presence was not with Israel. False worship stagnates your spiritual walk and hinders your prayers. Gideon's conversation with the angel showed him what to do: return to the pattern of worship God gave to his ancestors. You see, there is almost always someone in a person's family who has been rightly aligned with God. As in Josiah's case, your godly example might have lived many generations before you. Perhaps no one in your family has ever been rightly aligned with God. You can change this by choosing to align with God's pattern of Kingdom worship, as Gideon did. Gideon offered a sacrifice to the Lord—in other words, he worshiped.

Demonic Cords

Demonic cords are a way the enemy operates against believers. You cannot afford to forget that the enemy works within a well-organized demonic framework of principalities, powers, rulers and spiritual wickedness in high places—places that are, according to *Strong's Concordance*, above the sky,[7] which is considered to be the second heaven. Demonic rankings are revealed in the descriptions of principalities, powers, rulers and spiritual wickedness in high places. This depicts a confederacy, and it indicates that demonic teams working together are like a three-strand cord. Though one may be overpowered, two can defend themselves, and a cord of three strands is not quickly broken. The enemy understands the power of teams to combine their forces to frustrate the believer. Within these teams is agreement; the demonic forces work together toward a common goal. This demonic picture shows the enemy working in a distorted manner, opposite to the intention of God.

> Two are better than one because they have a more satisfying return for their labor; for if either of them falls, the one will lift up his companion. But woe to him who is alone when he falls and does not have another to lift him up. Again, if two lie down together, then they keep warm; but how can one be warm alone? And though one can overpower him who is alone, two can resist him. A cord of three strands is not quickly broken.
>
> Ecclesiastes 4:9–12 AMP

Scripture declares that a cord of three strands is not easily broken. This refers to teamwork and unity. You probably have heard this Scripture quoted at a marriage ceremony as an exhortation to a new husband and wife to keep Jesus as their partner in the marriage. Wherever there is agreement, there is strength. The Bible gives us another image of the power of unity in Leviticus: "And you will chase your enemies, and they will fall before you by the sword. Five of you will chase a hundred, and a hundred of you will put ten thousand to flight; your enemies will fall before you by the sword" (Leviticus 26:7–8 AMP).

There is strength in numbers when there is unity. The enemy understands this, so each day you and I are subjected to the enemy's attacks. If the enemy can drive you from the place of prayer, he has been successful in disconnecting you from your

Holy Spirit power source. When this happens, failure is inevitable. When you encounter demonic resistance, find believers who are faithful to stand in faith, praying with you. This is the law of agreement Jesus taught. Finding other believers to agree with you in prayer is a key to destroying demonic carpenters. Though the enemy knows the power of unity, it is not stronger than the unity of believers.

> ### LAW OF AGREEMENT
>
> When two believers come into agreement about anything they ask within the will of God, it will be done by our Heavenly Father.

Again I say to you, that if two believers on earth agree [that is, are of one mind, in harmony] about anything that they ask [within the will of God], it will be done for them by My Father in heaven. For where two or three are gathered in My name [meeting together as My followers], I am there among them.

Matthew 18:19–20 AMP

We see an example of a demonic confederacy in the book of Judges, which shows clearly how such confederacies form threefold cords of wickedness. Themes of judgment, repentance and restoration recur throughout Judges. The enemies of the nation of Israel would often form alliances with other nations so that they might overcome Israel. An example is King Eglon, ruler of the Moabites, whom we will discuss more fully in chapter 9. To secure his victory over Israel, King Eglon formed a demonic alliance with two other long-standing enemies of Israel, the Amalekites and the Ammonites. The nation of Israel had been under judgment, serving Eglon for eighteen years. Prophetically, Eglon represents a sevenfold spirit of destruction, robbery, fear, murder, kidnapping, deception and delay.

The enemy operates from a position of pseudostrength—in other words, the enemy cannot overcome you. Therefore, he will form demonic alliances against you in order to frustrate your purpose. Operating in revelation is necessary for victory, for gaining revelation from heaven is key to overcoming your enemies. Through revelation, Holy Spirit will not only show you how the enemy is operating against you, He will also give you strategies for victory.

> ## APPLICATION
>
> Ask the Holy Spirit to show you how any demonic carpenters might be operating against you. Then ask the Holy Spirit to show you how heaven is moving on your behalf. Let the Holy Spirit reveal prayer strategies to dismantle any cords of wickedness that might be in operation.

Key Scriptures: Isaiah 54:15–17; Matthew 6:14–15; Judges 6:12–13; Ecclesiastes 4:9–12; Leviticus 26:7–8; Matthew 18:19–20

Key Points:

- Demonic carpenters are dark forces operating against you, trying to create a different reality for you than the one God intends.
- Demonic carpenters operate in a type of confederacy, which is defined as a league or compact for mutual support or common action.
- Demonic arrows are sent by the enemy into your life to pierce your soul. When you are offended or wounded in your soul in some manner, you must be careful to allow Holy Spirit to help you to forgive. Unforgiveness can be a

catalyst to the entrance of demonic carpenters into your life.

- Familial spirits, or generational iniquities, are passed down from generation to generation, often evidenced in issues like alcoholism, domestic violence, drug addiction, divorce, etc.
- We can choose to walk in righteousness rather than following ungodly patterns set by our forefathers.
- Demonic altars are established in a family or territory through false worship.
- Demonic cords are alliances formed by the kingdom of darkness to overcome believers.
- Law of forgiveness: Forgive and you will be forgiven.
- Law of agreement:

> Again I say to you, that if two believers on earth agree [that is, are of one mind, in harmony] about anything that they ask [within the will of God], it will be done for them by My Father in heaven. For where two or three are gathered in My name [meeting together as My followers], I am there among them.
>
> Matthew 18:19–20 AMP

Reflection: Ask the Lord to show you any areas of unforgiveness that you have not released to Him. Ask the Lord to show you any areas where familial spirits are hindering you.

CHAPTER FIVE

Breaking Cycles of Self-Sabotage

Jesus answered and said unto them, "Verily I say unto you, if ye have faith and doubt not, ye shall not only do this which is done to the fig tree, but also if ye shall say unto this mountain, 'Be thou removed and be thou cast into the sea,' it shall be done."

Matthew 21:21

While I was attending a conference, I heard a testimony given by a senior pastor whose church was situated on a stretch of land directly in front of a mountainous segment. At some point, the church's parking capacity became an issue, and the pastor recognized the need for a new parking lot. The adjoining land was not conducive to creating a parking lot since it was not flat. To level the land would require more funds than the church had available. One day the pastor read from Matthew 21:21, "If ye shall say unto this mountain, 'Be thou removed and be thou cast into the sea,' it shall be done." When the pastor read the passage, faith came alive in him. He began speaking Matthew 21:21 every day. He would drive to the church property and sit in his car, speaking Matthew 21:21 over the mountain. He spoke this Scripture so much that his children began to say it.

One day, while the pastor was in his office, a man came to see him. The man began, "Pastor, you need a new parking lot." The pastor responded, "I know, but we don't have money for a new parking lot." To which the man responded, "I didn't ask you if you had money. You need a new parking lot." It turned out that the man was a contractor. Some time later, the man showed up at the church with his crew, bulldozed the land into a flat surface and paved a new parking lot, free of charge. That is how God works. When you grab hold of faith in God's Word, you will have exactly what you say. Words have power, and when you speak in alignment with God's Word, you will see God's promises manifest.

The Power of Language

Our social order is based primarily on language; entire cultures are formed around a commonality of language, a phenomenon we see as far back as Genesis: "Now the whole earth spoke one language and used the same words (vocabulary). And as people journeyed eastward, they found a plain in the land of Shinar and they settled there" (Genesis 11:1–2 AMP). The power of language extends even further back, however, for God Himself used language to craft His creation. God had only to say, "Let there be light," and there was light. God used language to form almost all of creation. It was not until God created Adam and Eve—His masterpiece, created in the image and likeness of God—that He used nonverbal methods.

As creation developed, the centrality of language is demonstrated again and again. Adam learned language from hearing God talk to him. Adam's daily conversations with God cultivated his capacity to speak. I am sure Eve learned to speak by hearing God and Adam converse with each other and with her. All social cultures have since developed some form of language. Even animals communicate through a rudimentary form of language, though it differs drastically from human language.

I travel frequently as a minister, and a considerable amount of my travel is within the United States, a primarily English-speaking nation. Rarely have I encountered problems communicating in the United States, unless I am in a Spanish-speaking church. The ease with which I speak changes significantly when I travel internationally, for I often must use an interpreter. Some years ago, my late husband and I were traveling in Europe for ministry. During his sermon, my husband used a slang term that was common in the United States but unknown to the interpreter. He stopped interpreting and stared at my husband, who said the term again. After repeating it a third time, my husband recognized that it was unknown to the interpreter and used a different phrase to convey his point. Effective communicators understand that language is connected to the culture, and they find ways to communicate principles and concepts so that they can be understood by the hearer.

As Kingdom citizens, we operate the same way. We must understand God's system of communication. Like Adam, we learn to speak Kingdom language as we listen to God speak, and one way He speaks to us is through His Word. When we say what God has said about our situation, whatever we are speaking to must respond. Everything in earth and above earth has a language and responds to the words we speak. That pastor spoke to a plot of land that needed to be leveled for a new parking lot. What do you need to speak to? Are you speaking faith-filled words or words filled with doubt and unbelief? Remember, you have what you say—that is the law of language creativity. The enemy can gain access to your portion based on the words you speak.

> | APPLICATION
>
> Review your prayer list. What are you praying about that has not manifested? Commit to speaking faith over your prayer list each day.

The Language of Self-Sabotage

When I was completing my doctoral studies at the University of Wisconsin in Milwaukee, my program of study required me to take two classes in educational statistics. I have never been fluent in the language of mathematics, and I dreaded these classes. Not only did I dread them, I talked about how much I dreaded them each day. I did not think about the fact that my words were creating a reality for me; I just kept complaining about how much I hated statistics.

I was operating in self-sabotage. Self-sabotage can be defined as deliberately stopping yourself from achieving something or preventing a plan from being successful. I believe that self-sabotage can manifest either consciously or unconsciously. For example, conscious self-sabotage might manifest in addictive behavior or some other form of behavior that prevents an individual from excelling in life. Unconscious self-sabotage might manifest in negative self-talk—*I am so stupid. My prayers will never be answered. This situation is going to be the death of me.* I have heard people say such things. This kind of self-talk is counterproductive and not based in faith. When we speak words that are faith filled, heaven begins moving on our behalf. When we speak words that are not faith filled, we open the door to demonic activity in our lives. Each time I complained about educational statistics, I closed off part of my brain's processing capacity, making it difficult to retain information. Although I passed both courses, I am convinced that adhering to the practice of praying and decreeing God's Word over my capacity to retain statistical language would have made my journey easier. That is what happens when we speak negative words that work against us and not for us. Rather than saying what God says about our situation, we release words of doubt and frustration, empowering the enemy who is operating against us. That is self-sabotage. We are defeated by the words from our own lips.

One year I was having lunch with three friends during the Christmas season. At the conclusion of our meal, the waiter asked if there was anything else he could bring to us. My friends said no, but as the waiter turned to walk away, I stopped him. "Yes, there is something you can get for me." The waiter turned and asked me what he could bring me. I smiled and responded, "You can bring me four bills indicating no charge."

The waiter looked stunned, so I repeated my request with a smile. He indicated that he would see what he could do. My friends were as shocked by my boldness as the waiter. They could not believe that I had made such a request. I simply laughed. "You will have what you say!"

Several moments later the waiter returned with our bills, each in its own bill holder. As we each opened a holder to review our bills, we saw "No charge" written on each one. Now, I am not telling you to try this the next time you are out to eat. I am simply providing a real-life instance of heaven breathing on my words and manifesting my request. This incident was a manifestation of the law of language creativity. God uses our words, just as He did for Daniel: "From the very first day you decided to get wisdom and to be humble in front of God, he has been listening to your prayers. I came to you because you have been praying" (Daniel 10:12 ERV).

Heaven responds when you speak God's Word. When he did not receive an immediate response to his prayers, Daniel chose the path of faith. He did not spend each day murmuring and complaining. Daniel chose to worship God, and as a result, heaven moved on his behalf. When we pray, spiritual processes are put into motion that result in a response to us. In Daniel's case, a messenger angel was dispatched; after that, Michael, one of the warrior angels, was sent to contend against the demonic spirits in the second heaven who were creating a demonic blockage. The war lasted 21 days; God's angels prevailed and Daniel received his response. I believe that when we link our prayers to the Word of God and with faith, we assist heaven in breaking through on our behalf. You must gain a new perspective of how powerful you were created to be. When you do, you become unstoppable on earth. You soar to new heights in prayer, and in each season manifestation of your prayers and your portion is released.

Change Your Lens

There is an old fable about a farmer who loved his eagle and raised it with his chickens. One day, a man asked the owner, "Why is the eagle, proudest of all the birds, living in a barn with chickens?" The farmer, professing his affection for the eagle, answered that he provided all of the eagle's needs, so that it had no need of hunting or flying.

The passerby found this curious. He picked up the eagle and told it, "You belong to the sky and not to earth. Stretch forth your wings and fly." But the eagle merely rejoined the chickens. Again the man tried, this time bringing the eagle to the roof of its owner's house. Again the eagle returned to the chickens.

Finally, the man carried the eagle to the top of a mountain. The eagle was frightened, but with no way to get back down the mountain, it stretched its wings and began to fly toward the sun.

The moral? "The eagle had it in him all along. But his up-bringing and lack of belief in himself led to self-sabotage."[1]

Are you limiting yourself in a similar manner? Do you see yourself the way God sees you, or do you see yourself through a lens of self-sabotage? Like the man in the story, when he saw the eagle, he understood its majestic nature. He understood the eagle was created to soar in high places. Hell sees your Kingdom nature and knows that you were created to triumph over the powers of darkness. This is why hell uses trauma and unsolved issues in your life to create a negative self-image within you as a result of you speaking negative words against yourself. These words are a type of curse, which we release against our own lives. Another way to understand this concept can be found in the term *self-fulfilling prophecy*, referring to when a person unknowingly causes a prediction to come true due to the simple fact that he or she expects it to come true. In other words, an expectation about a subject, such as a person or event, can affect our behavior toward that subject, which causes the expectation to be realized.[2] The enemy cannot curse your life, but you are able to open the doors for curses to operate through words of unbelief. When you are frustrated, it is important that you pay attention to the things you say. After all, you are creating something with your words. Understanding how the spirit of self-sabotage works is a key to victory in this area. Here are some things to consider:

1. *Not understanding the power of your words.* I remember an old adage, "Loose lips sink ships." It is important that you govern your words and avoid negative self-talk. Rather than complaining or speaking negative words, learn to say what God says about your request.

2. *Lack of spiritual stamina.* Spiritual stamina means you have developed the capacity to worship, war and wait. If

you do not develop this capacity, you will quit praying when the warfare against you becomes more intense. A regular practice of prayer and worship helps you to build spiritual stamina.

3. *Fear of failure.* Negative self-talk can produce fear within you. When fear comes in, doubt and unbelief follow. God wants you to be victorious in every area of your life. He also wants you to possess your portion. Let this fact become part of the foundation you stand on.

4. *Not knowing the Word of God.* When you are not sure what you are asking for is in alignment with God's will, this can create double-mindedness within you. Praying the Scriptures is an effective foundation for praying and helps you to overcome in this area. Satan approached Eve with the question, *Has God really said?* You will experience similar attacks, but the Word of God helps you to overcome.

5. *Not knowing God's prophetic promises for you.* When you do not understand your portion, which is your inheritance, hell will attempt to seize it. Adam and Eve were given a garden to tend. You also have a garden, a portion, that God has given to you. Allow Holy Spirit to open your eyes to see your God-given portion.

6. *No revelation.* Without revelation, you will not receive strategies to overcome your enemy and see your portion returned. Prayer and worship create an atmosphere of faith within you and position you to receive revelation through the Spirit of God.

APPLICATION

Ask the Lord to show you any areas of your life where you are committing self-sabotage. Repent of these areas and receive strength and wisdom to move forward in faith.

Retribution is linked with the principle of interest, increase and multiplication. When any portion of your portion has been seized by hell, God requires interest to be paid upon the return of your goods. Hell is counting on your ignorance of this truth. Hell is also counting on your unwillingness to press into the depth and breadth of prayer necessary to receive revelation that secures the release of your portion. Overcoming your enemy is no walk in the park. This is why you need to align with heaven so that you overcome your enemy. I encourage you to use these prayers and prophetic decrees as you press through into breakthrough.

Lord Jesus, I repent for every word I have spoken against Your plans for my life. Because I repent, every spirit of shame and condemnation attempting to operate against me in this area must leave, in Jesus' name.

I pluck up every negative word that I have spoken that is trying to take root and grow. I use the power of Kingdom language and decree that it will not grow! As Jesus spoke to the fig tree and commanded it to wither and die, I speak to every word of self-sabotage that I have spoken, and I command every evil word to die.

Today I receive a sevenfold payback for everything taken from me and my family. By the authority and power that comes through the blood of Jesus, I command my enemies to return what was stolen from me and to pay sevenfold tribute to me.

Let God arise and all the enemies of my breakthrough be scattered in the name of Jesus.

Let the fire of God melt away the stones hindering my blessings, in the mighty name of Jesus.

Let the cloud blocking the sunlight of my glory and breakthrough be dispersed in the name of Jesus.

Lord, open my eyes and do not let the way before me be dark. Let me see what I have not been able to see before.

Let the eyes of my understanding be enlightened, according to Ephesians 1:18.

Lord, I ask that You rend the heavens and come down, causing favor, power, promotion, breakthrough, finances, good health, sound mind and peace to be released into my life.

Right now, I stand in my position as a child of God, ordained to reign as a king on earth. According to Your Word, I decree that the fragrance of divine favor covers me, and I have favor with God and man. God has put His word in my mouth as a weapon of destruction and restoration. I use that power to speak destruction upon all the devil's agents assigned to hinder me and divert my blessings. I use the same weapon to decree restoration upon my life, in Jesus' name.

||||||||||||||||||||||||||||||||||||||||||||||||||||||||||||||||||||||||||||||||||||||||||||||||||||||||||

Key Scriptures: Matthew 21:21; Daniel 10:12

Key Points: Negative self-talk is a weapon of sabotage that the enemy influences us to use against ourselves.

Reflection: Review the list of areas wherein self-sabotage might be operating. Ask the Lord to show you whether or not any of these issues might be operating and hindering your prayers.

CHAPTER SIX

The Spirit of Pisgah

Get thee up into the top of Pisgah, and lift up thine eyes westward, and northward, and southward, and eastward, and behold it with thine eyes: for thou shalt not go over this Jordan.

Deuteronomy 3:27 KJV

Waiting is something most of us are accustomed to. We wait in line at stores, gas stations and movie theaters. We wait in the doctor's office, in the hair salon or at the airport. Waiting is a part of life.

Delay, on the other hand, is something entirely different. To delay is to postpone or defer until later, or to cause to be later or slower than expected or desired. Delay begins the moment your wait should have been over, but it is not. When delay begins, you are in position for the next thing, but the next thing does not begin. For me, there is nothing more frustrating than delay. I spend considerable time traveling, which almost always involves sitting at the airport. I often arrive early and spend time reading or writing, which I am content to do. But when the airline announces a flight delay, my attitude changes. I am usually no longer content to write or read; I am ready to leave. The fact that I am delayed temporarily interrupts my creative processes and concentration. Delay has this effect. It is not just waiting; it is a holding pattern.

As a frequent traveler I have endured my share of airline departure delays. On one such occasion, the airline boarded everyone onto the plane. After the boarding door was closed, I noticed that the engine stopped running. There we sat, ready for departure, and the plane's engines were silent. A short time later, an announcement was made that the plane's starter was malfunctioning and needed repair. We were positioned for movement, but delay unexpectedly reared its head. This is a picture of how the spirit of delay operates. Everything appears to be in place, you are positioned for victory—and nothing happens. Take the women's conference I planned: We started out well, registrations were coming in, and suddenly we had come to a complete standstill. This can be frustrating.

While delay encompasses the act of waiting, the two are not the same. They may seem similar, but there are important distinctions. Waiting is defined as staying in place, with an expectation of something happening. Another dictionary defines to wait as remaining inactive, or in a state of repose, until something expected happens. Waiting includes the attitude of expectation, while delay does not. Delay implies the occurrence of an unexpected event beyond your control, which initiates the wait, but waiting implies the passage of time necessary for an event to occur.

In other words, we wait expectantly for manifestation, which does not necessarily mean delay; but when waiting is caused by delay, we are experiencing an unauthorized event. That is the *spirit of Pisgah*, or the spirit of delay. When you are believing and waiting for responses to your prayers, you must discern the reason your responses have not manifested.

Obedience

In Numbers 20, Moses was commanded to speak to a rock to bring forth water for the people of Israel, who repeatedly complained whenever they experienced a food or water shortage. God gave Moses a specific command: "Speak to the rock in front of the people. Then water will flow from the rock" (verse 8 ERV).

Moses decided not to listen. In response to yet another season of complaining by Israel, Moses instead chided the people for their tendency to complain. "Now listen to me. I will cause water to flow from this rock" (verse 10 ERV). Moses then struck the rock twice. This is not what God had instructed him to do. In every season of your life, God will give you strategies and instructions to bring forth your provision. Like Moses, you can choose to obey or to disobey.

Jericho was a portion of Israel's inheritance, and God gave Israel His strategy to bring the nation into possession of their portion. That is how revelation works. God communicates a clear strategy that results in victory, if we obey. God's strategy for Israel was seven priests leading the march and blowing trumpets, with other priests carrying the Ark of God's presence. Soldiers bearing weapons marched in front of the priests blowing the trumpets. Everyone else marched behind the priests carrying the Ark. They did this once every day for six days. They were instructed not to speak during the march; they simply marched around Jericho once each day for six days, fully armed but voices silent.

Can you imagine the ridicule they might have endured during those six days? I am sure some who were marching were wondering why they were marching rather than fighting. I imagine they wondered why they were not permitted to release a war cry. Is it possible that each day they marched around Jericho, the people inside the walls were mocking them? Maybe they were throwing rocks at the processional. No matter what distraction came from inside the walls, Israel remained focused, carrying out God's instructions. On the seventh day, Israel prepared to march around Jericho as they had done the previous six days; today, however, they would march around seven times, with priests blowing their trumpets. On that seventh day, Joshua commanded Israel to release a war cry. When they did, the walls of Jericho fell flat. The city was delivered into Israel's hands. Was it the simple act of marching and blowing trumpets that caused the city to be given into Israel's hands? No. It was their obedience to the strategy God had given them, which released heaven to move on their behalf.

Moses had violated the principle of obedience when he struck the rock instead of speaking to it. The penalty Moses faced was to ascend Mount Pisgah to view the Promised Land, but to not be allowed to enter. The spirit of Pisgah is the spirit of "almost there." You are so close to breakthrough—and then failure happens. You have applied for a job for which you are qualified. After multiple interviews, you are informed that someone else has been selected. Almost there! Your ministry starts to increase, and just as suddenly as growth begins, it stops. Almost there! You feel led to convene a conference or some other type of gathering. Registration starts off fine and suddenly stops, leaving you without a sufficient number of attendees. Almost there! Maybe you are in treatment for a medical condition. Your physician reports improvement, and then suddenly, you are worse. Almost there!

Moses had led Israel out of Egypt and through the wilderness for forty years. He had watched a generation die in the wilderness, and finally their descendants were preparing to cross over into the Promised Land. Moses was almost there! When failure happens in our lives at the point of "almost there," the enemy uses these events to taunt us. "Has God really said?" Rather than coming into agreement with hell, keep yourself in agreement with God. Keep walking around the situation in prayer. Keep decreeing the Word of God. Keep worshiping. If God has said yes, hell has to let go of your portion.

> APPLICATION
>
> How do you see the spirit of delay operating in your life? What has not manifested yet?

Purposed Waiting

There are times that God responds, "Not yet," to something you request in prayer. This indicates a time of waiting that God can use to develop patience in you. The usual Hebrew expression for patience is related to the verb meaning "to be long," and it involves the idea of "being long" to become riled, or slow to become angry. Two different Greek words are translated with the word *patience*: One has the idea of remaining firm under tests and trials and is better translated as "endurance" or "steadfastness." The other Greek word is related to the above Hebrew meaning and defines patience as "long-spiritedness" or "calmness of spirit," even under severe provocation to lose one's temper.[1] Patience is a fruit of the Spirit developed in you. We say things like, "You need to learn patience." It is God, however, who develops the capacity to wait patiently by allowing us to be in situations in which waiting is required. This is a legal time of waiting; God is working something in you. He is creating capacity within you.

The Finishing Anointing

The ultimate goal of the enemy is not simply to stop your progress, but for you to experience failure when you are at the point of success. This happens to damage not only your credibility but the credibility of God. Maybe you are locked into a cycle in which failure at this point is normal. You see the goal, you are right on the edge of success in your endeavor, and suddenly, failure happens. When this occurs, a supernatural response is needed to break the cycle. Our prayer needs to be engaged in a way that allows success to manifest. Jesus operated in the "finishing" anointing, and we see the same anointing upon the apostle Paul: "I have fought an excellent fight. I have finished my full course and I've kept my heart full of faith" (2 Timothy 4:7 TPT).

God's plan for you is to finish your race. Each of us has been assigned a course of life. Just as God spoke to Jeremiah concerning His plan for Jeremiah's life, your life was planned before you were born.

> Before I formed you in the womb I knew you [and approved of you as My chosen instrument], and before you were born I consecrated you [to Myself as My own]; I have appointed you as a prophet to the nations.
>
> Jeremiah 1:5 AMP

God told Jeremiah that He knew him before he was born and planned a course of life for him as a prophet. Then He reiterated His plan to Jeremiah later in life when things were difficult. The nation of Israel was in the midst of God's judgment, as evidenced by war and Babylonian captivity. God wanted Israel to know their captivity would end after seventy years, for He did not want Israel to lose hope for their future. "'I know the plans and thoughts that I have for you,' says the LORD, 'plans for peace and well-being and not for disaster, to give you a future and a hope'" (Jeremiah 29:11 AMP).

Before Jeremiah was born, God planned a good future for him. It was the plan of God that Jeremiah would be successful in his ministry assignment. It is God's desire that you will be successful in the ministry assignment He has given you. When I speak of ministry, I am including all types of ministry, whether you are called to church leadership, outreach, business or your family. God desires for you to be successful. To be successful means you are fulfilling the purpose assigned to your life, and you are living out your destiny.

We are all drawn to successful people. No one wants to hear the story of how someone became a failure; what we really want to know is how someone became successful. We want to know what they did. What steps did they take that culminated in their success? How were they able to grow their businesses into *Fortune 500* companies? While it is good to hear the testimonies of successful people because we can be inspired and learn from them, God's plan for you is found in His Word. "The LORD will accomplish that which concerns me; Your [unwavering] loving kindness, O LORD, endures forever" (Psalm 138:8 AMP).

God is committed to accomplishing His will on earth. As Kingdom citizens, we are called to carry out God's agenda on earth. God has not planned failure for you. He positions you to win. God desires that you finish your race and not just finish—He wants you to finish strong. Take a moment to pray this simple prayer.

Lord, I thank You that I am anointed to finish. I dismiss every assignment of delay that is attempting to hinder my prayers. Lord, I thank You that heaven is warring with me. The angelic host has been released to bring me to the place of finishing. Not only will I finish, I will finish strong, in Jesus' name.

The Matter of Focus

As you align with God's plan for your life and move through the time of waiting, focus is a vital key. Do not allow yourself to become distracted. Whenever I have approached a season of transition, distraction is a weapon the enemy attempts to use against me. Focus on God's assignment for me at that time has proven to be the weapon to overcome spirits of distraction. During this time, as you refuse to accept anything other than God's plan for your life, you will experience more answers to your prayers.

> He came to Bethsaida, and they brought a blind man unto Him, and besought Him to touch him. And He took the blind man by the hand, and led him out of the town. And when He had spit on his eyes and put His hands upon him, He asked him if he saw anything. And he looked up and said, "I see men as trees, walking." After that He put His hands again upon his eyes and made him look up; and he was restored, and saw every man clearly.
>
> Mark 8:22–25

Loss of focus is directly connected to our ability to see and comprehend. Jesus was traveling through a town when a blind man was brought before Him. In his original state, this man totally lacked sight; he was blind. He had no capacity to see. What is interesting in this passage is the fact that the blind man did not ask for healing himself. Those who led him to Jesus asked Jesus to heal him. Having friends who are discerning and who can encourage us forward in life is important. It is how we move in the law of agreement.

> Again, I give you an eternal truth: If two of you agree to ask God for something in a symphony of prayer, my heavenly Father will do it for you. For wherever two or three come together in honor of my name, I am right there with them!
>
> Matthew 18:19–20 TPT

| LAW OF AGREEMENT |

Biblical prayer with other believers brings a response from God.

This man did not ask to be taken to Jesus; neither did he ask for healing. His friends asked on his behalf. The blind man also did not refuse to go to Jesus for his healing, which means he was in agreement. When we stand in prayer with other believers, God responds. This is the law of agreement. Do you have friends to encourage you in prayer and help you connect to the Lord? Do you have friends who are able to join you in contending against demonic forces intent on frustrating your prayer efforts? If not, ask the Lord to bring friends into your life who can provide prayer support to you, especially when you are contending with the spirit of delay.

We can see several other key factors in the account of the blind man of Bethsaida:

- Jesus removed the man from his familiar environment, leading him by the hand out of town. Sometimes you need to change your prayer strategy. We often fall into a routinized way of prayer. While consistency and routine can be good, when you are overcoming the spirit of Pisgah, you need to break out of routine.
- Jesus used an unusual method to bring healing to this man; He spit on his eyes. When you are experiencing delay, you must gain sight. God will allow you to see the reason your prayers have not manifested. If you are waiting, God may be developing patience in you. Remember, patience is a fruit of the Spirit. If you are dealing with delay, God will give you revelation, or discernment, concerning what is happening in the spiritual realm.

- Focus matters. It seems the man's friends understood more than the blind man how badly he needed his sight. Jesus responded by spitting on the man's eyes and asking him if he could see anything. After Jesus spit on the man's eyes, he had sight, but he did not have clarity—he lacked focus. Focus is the ability not just to see but to see clearly, to have clear visual definition. In prayer, you need clear visual definition.

- Clarity can be progressive. The level of clarity needed did not come after Jesus spit on the man's eyes. The man reported he saw men as trees walking. This means he could see but lacked clarity. After the second touch, not only was the man no longer blind, he had the clarity of sight he needed. The more time you spend in prayer, the more visual definition you will have. In other words, your clarity will become clearer.

The spirit of Pisgah is designed to keep you on the verge of breakthrough. It is the place of "almost there." It is also movement without manifestation. Recently, God spoke this prophetic word to me.

This is the season that I am breaking the cycle of movement with no manifestation; it is a revolving door cycle. My Church keeps moving, but they are only going in circles. My Church has now come into the season of manifestation! The Church will now begin experiencing rapid responses to their prayers.

When you spend time praying but do not see manifestation, it could be that you are being opposed by the spirit of delay. This is what happened to Daniel, who prayed 21 days before he received a response. He did not get discouraged after a few days; he kept praying until a response came. This is what you must do—keep praying and believing.

> APPLICATION
>
> Find other believers to stand with you in prayer. Let the Lord give you revelation as to why you have not received a response. Waiting works to your benefit, but delay comes to frustrate you. It is important to know the difference.

Lack of focus prevents you from having a clear sense of direction. Another way to see this issue is understanding time wasters. You can expend your efforts in prayer in ways that are not productive because you lack focus. You do not see the prayer strategy that will bring you into victory. Through prayer, worship and meditation on God's Word, your focus is sharpened, and time wasters are eliminated. Only intentional prayer sharpens our focus and eliminates time wasters. Through prayer and worship, we not only receive revelation, but our focus is renewed to see what is hindering us and strategies to move forward. Lack of focus is a measure of diminished visual capacity. As you press into God's presence, your focus is sharpened, allowing you to see clearly.

> LAW OF FOCUS
>
> A lack of focus opens the door for time wasters to operate in your life. Focus eliminates time wasters.

These prayers and prophetic decrees can help you dismantle demon forces trying to limit you and keep you in the place of "almost there."

Lord, I ask that just as the eyes of the blind man were healed and his focus sharpened, let my focus be restored today, resulting in a renewed perspective. Let me see what I have not been able to see, in Jesus' name.

All spiritual wickedness in the second heavens fortified against me and my destiny today is put to shame, in the name of Jesus.

I decree the blood of Jesus over my life and over my destiny, in the name of Jesus.

I bind every power cursing my destiny into ineffectiveness and frustrating my purpose, in the name of Jesus.

Let chaos and confusion be released against every evil power trying to capture my blessing, in the name of Jesus.

I decree the blood of Jesus against every assignment of "almost there" operating in my life and my ministry. I will not have movement without manifestation. This year, God's promises manifest in my life, in my family and in my ministry.

|||||||||||||||||||||||||||||||||||||||||||||||||||||||||||||||||||||||||||||||||||||||||||||||

Key Scriptures: Deuteronomy 3:27; Jeremiah 1:5; Mark 8:22–25; Matthew 18:19–20

Key Points:
- Law of agreement: Biblical prayer with other believers brings a response from God.
- Law of focus: Only focused prayer will increase your capacity to see and eliminate time wasters.

Reflection: What are some areas where you can see the spirit of Pisgah (delay) operating in your life? Are there any areas of your life where God is asking for obedience and you have not submitted to Him yet?

_____

_____

_____

CHAPTER SEVEN

Hindrances to Prayer

I say to you, ask and keep on asking, and it will be given to you; seek and keep on seeking, and you will find; knock and keep on knocking, and the door will be opened to you. For everyone who keeps on asking [persistently], receives; and he who keeps on seeking [persistently], finds; and to him who keeps on knocking [persistently], the door will be opened.

Luke 11:9–10 AMP

As an educator of young children, I cultivated the practice of observing children at play with other children or interacting with their parents. Watching those interactions can be informative and amusing. Standing in the checkout line at the grocery store is a great place to watch children interact with their parents, because it is the treasure aisle of candy bars and other goodies. It is also the last line of negotiation for children who are trying to obtain a sweet prize. Children are convinced that winning the sweet prize, or whatever they want, is correlated to the frequency of asking. I'm sure that in the ears of the child, *no* sounds like *maybe*, and the possibility of getting the sweet prize prompts them to ask again. Over and over children ask, past the cashier and out the door, in many cases. These children believe if they ask and keep on asking, the sweet prize will be theirs. They seem to not get tired of asking. They are committed. This is a simple picture of what your attitude must be in prayer. You must ask and keep on asking, for God answers prayers.

As we have previously discussed, God's answers are yes, no and not yet. Because God is a good Father, He will not give His children anything that will harm them or something that does not agree with His nature and character. There are times when God is building capacity in us or developing the fruit of the Spirit in us. During these times He sovereignly activates a season of waiting. The time of waiting can be different for every believer and is dependent on the time for God's work in us for that season to be completed. Sometimes our prayers involve others, and we might experience a waiting season as God prepares and positions others involved in His response to us. It is important to spend time worshiping the Lord so that you discern the reason you have not received a response to prayer.

As I discussed earlier, walking in the anointing to wait is critical. Waiting does not imply inactivity. During your waiting season, prayer, worship and meditation on the Word of God are important. When the waiting season, which is really a development time, is over, it is time then to see answers to your prayers. If there is no response, you need to seek the Lord to confirm that your waiting season is over. Remember, God is a good Father who delights in responding to the prayers of His children.

If your waiting season is over and you have not received a response to your prayers, you have entered a season of delay, operating through demonic structures designed to hinder and frustrate you. If there are certain issues in your life that are outside the will of God, you will need to surrender these areas to the Lord, so that your prayers are not hindered.

As for us, we have all of these great witnesses who encircle us like clouds. So we must let go of every wound that has pierced us and the sin we so easily fall into. Then we will be able to run life's marathon race with passion and determination, for the path has been already marked out before us.

Hebrews 12:1 TPT

In this passage, life is described as a marathon race. If we are going to pray effectively, seeing answers to our prayers, like marathon runners we must strip away all encumbrances. Marathon runners only wear what is necessary. Everything else is considered an unnecessary weight that can prevent them from being effective in their race. As you commit to seeing more of your prayers answered, there are numerous areas that should be considered when you are trying to identify possible hindrances to your prayers.

Hindrance #1: Inconsistency

"Now Jesus was telling the disciples a parable to make the point that at all times they ought to pray and not give up and lose heart" (Luke 18:1 AMP). Inconsistency in prayer can be a hindrance to seeing your prayers answered. These are some of the factors that can be involved with inconsistency:

1. *Unbelief.* Unbelief is a robbing spirit. When we operate from a position of unbelief we can experience feelings of anger toward God. Rather than waiting in joyful expectation and hope, we can be overcome with feelings of frustration and anger. During these times hell will attempt to enlarge itself over you in an attempt to discourage you from continuing in prayer.

104

2. *Laziness.* Consistency in prayer requires you to cultivate a daily prayer habit. I have often been amazed at the frequency of people who request prayer but are not willing to pray for themselves. They seem to think that it is just easier to find someone else to do the praying and believing for them, rather than developing a personal prayer habit. When you take time to pray daily, you are renewed in faith and strength to wait.

3. *Distractions.* I have often counseled individuals about feeling frustrated over their perceptions that God is not answering their prayers. In most cases, when I have asked about their prayer lives, they admit to being busy and not always taking the time to pray. Distractions and interruptions are a part of life, and we must allow Holy Spirit to help us deal with distractions in such a way that we consistently find time for prayer.

4. *Commitment.* Lack of commitment to cultivate a consistent prayer habit can be an indication of a lack of commitment to spiritual things. This can come from allowing the gardens of our souls to go untended. As a result, we operate more from our soul realms than from the leading of Holy Spirit. The Bible describes this as carnality. Often, in these cases, individuals express a lack of commitment to spiritual things, which leads to not seeing their prayers answered.

APPLICATION

Take time to review how you are spending your time each day. Ask Holy Spirit to show you areas of your life contributing to a pattern of inconsistency in prayer. When the Spirit of God shows you these areas, be faithful to surrender them.

Inconsistency is a form of double-mindedness that keeps us from seeing responses to our prayers. When you are inconsistent, you are halfhearted and wavering in prayer. Inconsistency is akin to weeds growing unchecked in your garden. At some point, the weeds will choke off any fruit that would have grown. Consistency in prayer is a key to seeing more of your prayers answered. "When you are half-hearted and wavering it leaves you unstable. Can you really expect to receive anything from the Lord when you're in that condition?" (James 1:7–8 TPT).

Lord, deliver me from any assignment of sin and spiritual laziness operating in my life. I repent and surrender to You. Let my eyes be opened to see any assignment of hell operating behind any problem in my life. I receive freedom today, in Jesus' name.

Hindrance #2: Disobedience

"Loving me empowers you to obey my commands" (John 14:15 TPT). Love for God is a catalyst to obedience. When we consistently walk in disobedience, we do not operate in the measure of faith to see restoration and retribution released on our behalf, resulting in inconsistency.

Lord, let my eyes be opened to any area of disobedience operating in my life. I receive strength through Holy Spirit to surrender my will and desires under the authority and guidance of Holy Spirit, in Jesus' name.

Hindrance #3: Wrong Motives

"What is the cause of your conflicts and quarrels with each other? Doesn't the battle begin inside of you as you fight to

106

have your own way and fulfill your own desires?" (James 4:1 TPT). Our prayers must align with the Word of God, and the motivations of our hearts must be pure. Asking God to bless you with a new vehicle to "one up or keep up" with your neighbor or family member is an example of impure motives. Some years ago, I met a couple who were prospering in their lives. God's blessings were upon this family. At some point, though, the wife allowed demon spirits to taunt her with thoughts that everyone else in the church was prospering beyond her family. A spirit of discontentment began operating against her, resulting in her never being satisfied with the blessings God had given her family. Lust for things and pride, partnered with discontentment, resulted in the couple's debt load ballooning beyond their ability to pay. This is an example of how wrong motives can operate.

Let the lamp of Holy Spirit shine in my heart today. Examine every motive of my heart. Purify my desires so that I will love what You love and hate what You hate, in Jesus' name.

Hindrance #4: Personal Sin

If I had closed my eyes to my sin, the Lord God would have closed his ears to my prayer.

Psalm 66:18 TPT

If you cover up your sin you'll never do well. But if you confess your sins and forsake them, you will be kissed by mercy.

Proverbs 28:13 TPT

But if we freely admit our sins when his light uncovers them, he will be faithful to forgive us every time. God is just to forgive us our sins because of Christ, and he will continue to cleanse us from all unrighteousness.

1 John 1:9 TPT

Spending time in devotional prayer positions you to hear Holy Spirit speak to you concerning any sin issues in your life. You must be willing to hear clearly and obey quickly. Surrender these areas to the Lord, and receive His strength to help you live victoriously. The enemy looks for areas in our lives that are not surrendered to the Lord so that he might gain an opportunity to bring condemnation and shame into our lives. When condemnation and shame enter our lives, they rob us of faith.

"The ruler of this dark world is coming. But he has no power over me, for he has nothing to use against me. I am doing exactly what the Father destined for me to accomplish" (John 14:30–31 TPT). Jesus lived in submission to the Father's will. As a believer you are empowered by Holy Spirit to live in submission to the Father's will, also. Submit any personal sin issues to the Lord so that your prayers are not hindered.

I repent of any sin in my life and surrender myself, body, mind and spirit, to the authority of God, in Jesus' name.

Hindrance #5: Unforgiveness and Bitterness

"Be kind and affectionate toward one another. Has God graciously forgiven you? Then graciously forgive one another in the depths of Christ's love" (Ephesians 4:32 TPT). Unforgiveness is a robbing spirit. When you harbor unforgiveness in your heart, you are robbed of joy and vision because your focus is on the wrong done to you. When unforgiveness continues in your life, it grows, becoming a root of bitterness. Do not allow your spirit to become bitter; let the Spirit of God help you to forgive.

Lord, deliver me from any grudges, bitterness and unfor-giveness harbored against anyone for any reason. Let my vision be renewed to see You and not the offenses against me, in Jesus' name.

Hindrance #6: Unsurrendered Will

So then, surrender to God. Stand up to the devil and resist him and he will turn and run away from you. Move your heart closer and closer to God, and he will come even closer to you. But make sure you cleanse your life, you sinners, and keep your heart pure and stop doubting. Feel the pain of your sin, be sorrowful and weep! Let your joking around be turned into mourning and your joy into deep humiliation.

James 4:7–9 TPT

Our will must be surrendered to God daily. Jesus taught His disciples to pray, "Not my will, but Your will be done." Living dependent on God each day is the most effective way to prevent your will from rising above the will of God for you. Fasting can help to overcome stubborn areas of your will in which you might have difficulty surrendering. I encourage you to make this declaration over your life today:

I am redeemed through the blood of Jesus, and I surrender myself totally to God. As a blood-washed, blood-bought citizen of God's Kingdom, I come under the authority of God's Kingdom and none other.

Hindrance #7: Unresolved Conflict with Others

Forgiveness, patience, kindness and love are the most effective ways to overcome conflicts with others. Be quick to reconcile with those you are experiencing conflict with, including your spouse.

Now let me speak to the wives. Be devoted to your own husbands, so that even if some of them do not obey the Word of God, your kind conduct may win them over without you saying a thing. For when they observe your pure, godly life before God, it will impact them deeply. Let your true beauty come from your inner personality, not a focus on the external.

1 Peter 3:1–4 TPT

Husbands, you in turn must treat your wives with tenderness, viewing them as feminine partners who deserve to be honored, for they are co-heirs with you of the "divine grace of life," so that nothing will hinder your prayers.

1 Peter 3:7 TPT

This is how I want you to conduct yourself in these matters. If you enter your place of worship and, about to make an offering, you suddenly remember a grudge a friend has against you, abandon your offering, leave immediately, go to this friend and make things right. Then and only then, come back and work things out with God.

Matthew 5:23–24 MESSAGE

I do not wrestle with flesh and blood. My enemy operates from the second heaven. I loose myself from any conflict or resentment for others operating against my life, my family or my ministry. I speak peace and good relationships over my life, in Jesus' name.

Hindrance #8: Ignorance

I have previously discussed ignorance and the ways the kingdom of darkness seeks to frustrate our prayers through the veil of ignorance. One of the goals of demonic structures is to cover your gift, which is connected to your inheritance. When we operate in ignorance, we do not know God's heart for us in a given situation. When we do not know, demons will seek to suggest something that is not true ("Did God really say . . . ?"). If demons can convince you that perhaps God did not say, the portion they are covering will not be released. Revelation is light. When God's Word comes into us, light comes, and light dispels darkness. Not only that, whatever the enemy of your soul is trying to cover is exposed. Knowing God's will through His Word is vital if you are going to overcome ignorance. "As people understand your word, it brings light to their lives" (Psalm 119:130 ERV).

I do not operate in ignorance. I operate in the wisdom of the Kingdom of God in every area of my life. Every place of darkness being covered by the enemy, attempting to hide my blessings, is being illuminated by the light of God. Today I receive revelation to see in a new way.

||||||||||||||||||||||||||||||||||||||||||||||||||||||||||||||||||||||||||||||||||||||||||

Key Scriptures: Luke 11:9–10; Luke 18:1; John 14:15; James 4:1; Psalm 66:18; Ephesians 4:32; James 4:7–9; Psalm 119:130

Key Points: We must identify any issues in our lives that are hindering answers to more of our prayers.

- Hindrance #1: Inconsistency. Unbelief is a robbing spirit which produces inconsistency in you. Distractions, laziness and lack of commitment are produced through unbelief.
- Hindrance #2: Disobedience. When we continually walk in disobedience, we do not operate in the measure of faith needed to see more answers to our prayers.
- Hindrance #3: Wrong motives. Our motives must be pure and align with the Word of God.

- Hindrance #4: Personal sin. God is faithful and forgives our sin. Unrepented sin is a hindrance to your prayers.

- Hindrance #5: Unforgiveness and bitterness. These are also robbing spirits. When we refuse to forgive others, we hinder the flow of God's power in our lives and prevent more responses to our prayers.

- Hindrance #6: Unsurrendered will. Not surrendering certain areas of our lives to the Lord is an indicator of pride, stubbornness and rebellion against God's will.

- Hindrance #7: Unresolved conflict with others. The fruits of the Spirit—patience, love, forgiveness, kindness—are ways God's people resolve conflict. As you learn to walk in the Spirit, you will also learn to overcome conflicts with others.

- Hindrance #8: Ignorance. Ignorance is a key weapon the enemy uses against us. When we read God's Word, worship and pray, we create a flow of the anointing within us. The flow of anointing brings revelation light, causing us to overcome ignorance.

Reflection: Looking at the hindrances to prayer, are there any areas where the Holy Spirit is speaking to you? Take a moment to list the areas, and write a brief response to the Lord.

_____

_____

_____

_____

_____

CHAPTER EIGHT

The Power of Faith

Now faith brings our hopes into reality and becomes the foundation needed to acquire the things we long for. It is all the evidence required to prove what is still unseen.

Hebrews 11:1 TPT

My late husband, Bill, would often give a testimony of faith about an event that occurred early in his Kingdom walk. In those days, Bill did not own an automobile and usually traveled by city bus. It had been warm and sunny when Bill left his apartment that morning, and he had not taken an umbrella or jacket with him. On his way home, he decided to forego the bus ride, choosing instead to enjoy the weather and walk the two miles or so back to his apartment. Suddenly, the sky darkened, and Bill knew that rain was imminent. Here he was, quite a distance from home without jacket or umbrella, and the path he had chosen to walk was not along the bus route. He could tell that a heavy downpour was coming.

So Bill began to pray. He asked the Lord to hold the rain until he got home. As he continued walking, Bill began thanking the Lord for holding back the rain for him. Bill knew that God saw him that day walking home without a jacket or umbrella. He recounted to me that he knew God did not want him to be soaked in the rain. Each step Bill took was a step of faith. The skies were dark, the smell of rain was in the air and Bill was thanking God for not letting it rain until he arrived at his destination. Twenty minutes after his initial prayer asking the Lord to hold back the rain, Bill walked up to his apartment and onto the porch. It was as though the moment his feet were planted on the porch, the signal for rain to fall was released in the atmosphere. The downpour began suddenly, and not one drop of rain had fallen on Bill. This is an example of how faith operates.

| LAW OF FAITH |

God's supernatural ability working in us to believe is a key to seeing more of your prayers answered.

Faith operates in time and place. One of the best books I have read on faith is *Prayers That Outwit the Enemy* by Chuck D. Pierce and Rebecca Wagner Sytsema. It is full of wisdom to help you to understand faith, such as in this passage:

> Faith is that conviction, confidence, trust and belief that we have in an object or person. Everyone has faith to some degree. But what causes our faith as believers to be different is that our object is God Himself. . . . Faith is the persuasion given to us by God that the things we have not yet seen, we will see. Faith is the pause between what God has said He will do and our seeing Him act upon His word.[1]

Another way to understand faith is as God's capacity working within us to see what He has promised as though it were

114

already accomplished. As believers, we have each been given a measure of faith. In Scripture, the word *measure* is translated from the Greek word *metron* and means "portion."[2] You have been given a portion of faith, God's ability working in you to believe that He will answer your prayers. That is supernatural!

To further understand this, Chuck Pierce describes seven issues of faith:[3]

1. *Faith is linked with covenant.* In Genesis 15, God made a covenant with Abram and promised him an heir, though Abram and Sarai were well beyond childbearing years. More than twenty years later, God's promise to Abram and Sarai was fulfilled.

2. *Faith is linked with our vision and destiny.* Faith is a supernatural ability to see beyond what currently exists. Without faith, we do not have vision, since faith is the ability to "see."

3. *Faith comes from listening to the God with whom we have a relationship.* Hearing God's voice during our times of prayer and reading God's Word, the Bible, releases His voice to work in our lives.

4. *Faith works from our love.* God is pure love. Everything we do must be motivated by love for God. Without love, true faith cannot operate.

5. *Faith is based on our understanding of authority.* The centurion in Matthew 8 understood authority. Faith cannot operate in our hearts when we are resistant to authority.

6. *Faith must be demonstrated.* Faith results in manifestation. Whatever we are believing for will be seen in time. This is why the spirit of delay must be overcome.

7. *Faith can be increased.* As we grow in our walk with the Lord, trusting Him and believing for responses to our prayers, our capacity to believe expands.

Elements of Faith

And without faith living within us it would be impossible to please God. For we come to God in faith knowing that he is real and that he rewards the faith of those who give all their passion and strength into seeking him.

Hebrews 11:6 TPT

Faith, then, is birthed in a heart that responds to God's anointed utterance of the Anointed One.

Romans 10:17 TPT

For we walk by faith, not by sight [living our lives in a manner consistent with our confident belief in God's promises].

2 Corinthians 5:7 AMP

But the fruit produced by the Holy Spirit within you is divine love in all its varied expressions: joy that overflows, peace that subdues, patience that endures, kindness in action, a life full of virtue, faith that prevails, gentleness of heart, and strength of spirit. Never set the law above these qualities, for they are meant to be limitless.

Galatians 5:22–23 TPT

Faith is a fruit of the Spirit, a gift of the Spirit and a weapon given to us for war. Faith as a fruit of the Spirit is grown and developed over time. As you walk with the Lord, watching how He responds to your prayers, your capacity to believe increases. The more your capacity increases, the more you become a formidable opponent against demon forces that come against you. It is important that faith be developed in you. Without faith you cannot prevail over the powers of darkness attempting to hold back your portion.

We experience multiple attacks against our faith because faith is a powerful weapon against the powers of darkness. This was how hell was able to overcome Eve in the Garden. The whisper of Satan produced seeds of doubt in Eve, causing her to believe that God was withholding something good from her. That is typical of how hell works against our faith. In an attempt to damage our faith, the enemy uses well-timed attacks of murmuring, complaining and self-pity, resulting in us becoming more self-centered than God-centered. Satan will also delay our prayers while tempting us to react in anger and bitterness, which hardens our hearts before the Lord so that we cannot approach Him in faith.

When we lack faith, we lack vision. Vision is connected to our future. Without vision, we cannot see the portion God is bringing to us. In Psalm 68:19 (NKJV), David sang, "Blessed be the Lord, who daily loads us with benefits." Doubt robs us of joy and expectation of God's daily benefits, deepening the root of unbelief. When I experience a setback, I ask the Lord to help me guard my words. Often during setbacks, our faith is attacked by demon forces working against us, causing us to speak words that are not filled with faith. When we speak words that do not align with the Word of God, we experience greater adversity. When we complain, we create cursing rather than blessing. Our words are that powerful.

Lord, I thank You for the portion You have given to me. I repent for any words I have spoken that are not aligned with Your words. I decree that all adversity released into my life from words I have spoken is broken, and every dark force operating against me ceases its operations now, in Jesus' name.

The Gift of Faith

Now there are diversities of gifts, but the same Spirit. And there are differences of administrations, but the same Lord. And

117

there are diversities of operations, but it is the same God who worketh all in all. But the manifestation of the Spirit is given to every man to profit thereby: For to one is given by the Spirit the word of wisdom; to another the word of knowledge by the same Spirit; to another faith by the same Spirit.

1 Corinthians 12:4–9

In 1 Corinthians 12:1, the apostle Paul instructs the church in Corinth concerning spiritual things. He warns the believers, "Don't be ignorant." In other words, do not be without understanding of spiritual things.[4] God has given us spiritual gifts, God's supernatural ability operating in us, to accomplish Kingdom purposes. The gift of faith is the supernatural ability to believe God's Word and promises in difficult situations. I have seen that many who operate in the gift of miracles and healings also operate in the gift of faith. Chuck Pierce writes,

The gift of faith is a supernatural manifestation of a holy God within our spirit man. It is an instant impartation of faith with regard to a specific need. . . . The gift of faith goes beyond natural faith and saving faith into supernatural trust. When we have supernatural trust, no doubt can shake us from what we have heard.[5]

If you are going to see more of your prayers answered, experience restoration and go beyond to seeing retribution manifest on your behalf, you will need to operate in the gift of faith. Put to use the following strategies to help you begin to operate in the gift of faith:

1. Change your mind by receiving the mind of Christ according to Philippians 2:5–8.

118

2. Allow Holy Spirit to show you areas of unforgiveness or any toxic emotions in your heart. Let the Spirit of God help you to release those who have wounded you.

3. Change your atmosphere and speak faith. I have always found it difficult to be in the company of people who consistently complain. It feels as though all of the joy and peace is pulled from the atmosphere. Speaking faith-filled words fills the atmosphere with joy and hope. Remember the law of language creativity: You will have what you say. Speak the Word of the Lord over your situation and expect God to move on your behalf!

4. Guard your heart. Do not allow hope deferred to capture your heart. Hope deferred is a robbing spirit that blocks your faith. Continuing in worship, prayer and thanksgiving will keep your faith active and move you into a "suddenly" moment, when manifestation takes place on your behalf.

5. Let your capacity be increased. Overcoming is simply learning to come up and go over obstacles. This is a war process. Learning to war into your promise is necessary if you are going to see more of your prayers answered. As you war in faith, your capacity is increased. Allow the Spirit of God to shift you beyond your last place.

6. Develop a Kingdom mentality. Matthew 11:12 says, "The Kingdom of Heaven suffereth violence, and the violent take it by force." Seeing more of your prayers answered, experiencing restoration, going beyond and experiencing retribution will require you to develop a Kingdom mentality. This is spiritual warfare—taking up your God-given promises and not backing down. It is praying until your manifestation occurs. "In every battle, take faith as your wrap-around shield, for it is able to extinguish

119

the blazing arrows coming at you from the Evil One!"
(Ephesians 6:16 TPT).

I make the following decree over you today:

*I decree that new dimensions of faith are being released
in you. Every assignment of frustration that has come
against you is now broken, in Jesus' name. I speak strength
over you to war, fight and prevail over every enemy of
your provision. I activate a new season of manifestation
in your life, shifting you beyond restoration into retribution. Like David, you will pursue, overtake and recover
all!*

In the same way, I encourage you to make these decrees over
your life daily:

*I speak to every evil power holding back my blessings and
I command you to let go, in Jesus' name.*

*I speak to every demon of discouragement, and I com-
mand you to leave my life, in Jesus' name.*

*I command every demonic whispering spirit to be silent,
in Jesus' name.*

*My ears are filled with revelation. I hear what the Spirit
is saying to me.*

*My eyes are filled with Kingdom vision for my life, family,
business and ministry.*

*I will only speak words aligned with God's Word, words
of faith and hope, in Jesus' name.*

Today I receive a fresh release of the anointing of the overcomer upon my life, in my family, business and ministry, in Jesus' name.

||||||||||||||||||||||||||||||||||||||||||||||||||||||||||||||||||||||||||||||||||||||||||||

Key Scriptures: Hebrews 11:1; 1 Corinthians 12:4–9; Ephesians 6:16

Key Points: Law of faith: God's supernatural ability working in us to believe is a key to seeing more of our prayers answered.

Reflection: Looking at the strategies for operating in the gift of faith, what areas are strongest in your life? What areas are weaker and need to increase?

_____

_____

_____

_____

_____

CHAPTER NINE

War Strategies to Overcome Your Enemy

> Ehud made himself a sword with two sharp edges that was about 12 inches long. He tied the sword to his right thigh and hid it under his uniform.
>
> Judges 3:16 ERV

As you position yourself to seek the Lord, Holy Spirit will reveal war strategies to overcome your enemy. You must avoid trying to war through human wisdom; it is only through Kingdom revelation that you gain the proper strategies to defeat your enemies. Revelation opens your eyes to see the demonic alliance operating against you.

In addition to strategy, however, we also need a foundation for understanding the principles of biblical warfare, such as the principle of retribution. *Retribution* is a war term meaning recompense or reward; it is the dispensing or receiving of reward or punishment, or something given or exacted in recompense, especially punishment. Retribution is a principle of increase and multiplication. We can see this principle in 2 Thessalonians 1:6–8 (NASB), where the apostle Paul speaks of a future judgment against those who have afflicted and persecuted believers. That is the essence of retribution: God's judgment dispensed on behalf of His chosen ones.

When we speak of retribution, we are referring to more than getting back what was taken from us. That is restoration, or bringing back to a former position or condition. It is important to clarify the difference between restoration, reinstatement and retribution. The terms *restoration* and *reinstatement* are very similar, but they have a clear distinction: Restoration is reestablishment or bringing back into existence, and reinstatement means to restore to a former position or rank. Neither results in receiving more than what you had in the first place. Retribution, however, means exacting punishment on our enemies for taking our inheritance or delaying our blessings. Retribution is the full measure of restoration. When retribution is released on your behalf, you receive more than you had in the beginning, as though you were receiving interest.

My experience on a delayed flight due to the plane needing its starter replaced can help you understand retribution. After sitting on the plane for approximately thirty to forty minutes, we were instructed to deplane. I recognized that because I had been delayed, I should receive retribution. Restoration would mean simply getting to my destination. Retribution would mean compensation for my time. Immediately after I disembarked to begin waiting for another flight, I contacted the airline and requested compensation for the delay. This is an important part of retribution: If you do not pursue retribution, you are not likely to receive what is due to you. I doubt the airline would have given me any form of compensation for my inconvenience without my asking. Retribution is receiving compensation in the amount of up to seven times your loss. When I contacted the airline, I did not want a meal voucher; because I understood this spiritual principle, I was able to negotiate a significant compensation.

> **APPLICATION**
>
> Avoid trying to war through human wisdom; it is only through Kingdom revelation that you gain war strategies to defeat your enemies.

Obeying God's Strategy

From the time of their wandering in the desert, the Israelites had to contend with the Amalekites. The people of Amalek were descendants of Esau who had incurred the anger of God for their treatment of Israel during their exodus from Egypt.

> Don't forget what Amalek did to you on the road after you left Egypt, how he attacked you when you were tired, barely able to put one foot in front of another, mercilessly cut off your stragglers, and had no regard for God. When GOD, your God, gives you rest from all the enemies that surround you in the inheritance-land GOD, your God, is giving you to possess, you are to wipe the name of Amalek from off the Earth. Don't forget!
>
> Deuteronomy 25:17–19 MESSAGE

The Amalekites' treatment of Israel resulted in God's judgment. During Israel's exodus from Egypt, the Amalekites attacked those who lagged behind, primarily women and children. Because of this, God intended to revisit the sin of the Amalekites during the rule of King Saul, Israel's first king. God commanded Saul to totally destroy the Amalekites:

> This is the GOD-of-the-Angel-Armies speaking: "I'm about to get even with Amalek for ambushing Israel when Israel came

124

up out of Egypt. Here's what you are to do: Go to war against Amalek. Put everything connected with Amalek under a holy ban. And no exceptions! This is to be total destruction—men and women, children and infants, cattle and sheep, camels and donkeys—the works."

1 Samuel 15:2–3 MESSAGE

Rather than obey God, however, King Saul spared Agag, king of the Amalekites, and the best of the plunder. The Amalekites did not disappear from history at this point, as the Lord had intended; later in Israel's history, Hamon the Agagite (perhaps a descendant of King Agag), formed a wicked plan of genocide against the Israelites living in Persia.

In 1 Samuel 30, the Amalekites attempted to plunder King David by raiding Ziklag, a Judean village where David held property. The Amalekites burned the village and took captive all the women and children, including two of David's wives. (We see that the Amalekites followed a pattern of attacking those who are weaker and defenseless.) Both King David and King Saul received a prophetic word from God giving them war strategies to defeat the Amalekites. Saul did not follow God's directive and ultimately lost his kingdom; David, however, partnered with God as he implemented the war strategies God had given. He and his men defeated the Amalekites and rescued all the hostages. Not only did David recover all of the possessions that had been stolen, he and his men exacted retribution. Remember, retribution is more than the return of your stolen goods; retribution is the penalty the thief must pay for taking your goods in the first place. The spirit of Amalek is a robbing spirit that attempts to keep you in poverty, which is not God's will. God wants you to have enough provision, health and anointing to accomplish His will.

125

Defeating Israel's Enemies

In Matthew 12:43–45, we see a principle of deliverance: When an enemy is cast out, he always returns with reinforcements. This is what happened when Moab joined forces with the Ammonites and Amalekites against the tribes of Israel, who had recently settled in the Promised Land. The Moabites and Ammonites, who ruled east of the Jordan River, formed a demonic alliance with the Amalekites, a threefold cord of wickedness to overcome the nation of Israel. The Moabites and Ammonites were descendants of Lot, and the Ammonites were known for their cruelty in war—they were, as we would describe it today, war criminals. Whenever the Ammonites conquered a nation, their practice was to gouge out the right eyes of men who had been captured (see 1 Samuel 11:2) and cut open the stomachs of pregnant women (see Amos 1:13). The Ammonites worshiped Molech (see 1 Kings 11:7), a pagan god associated with child sacrifice, which was a common practice among Molech's worshipers.

Why was Israel subject to such wickedness? In Judges 3:12–14, we read of Israel turning away from the Lord to do evil. Israel's sin of idolatry resulted in forfeiture or loss of lands they had previously conquered, such as Jericho, known as the city of palms (see Deuteronomy 34:3). When you choose to follow cultural norms rooted in the spirit of the antichrist, you will suffer loss. *Antichrist* means to be against Christ. When you choose to not walk in alignment with God, you open the door for the enemy to return and reclaim that which you had started to possess.

God had supernaturally delivered Jericho into the hands of Israel following their seven-day walk around the city, after which the walls fell down. Yet later the city of palms was recaptured by Israel's enemies because of Israel's national disobedience to God. This is a picture of having no place to rest and no shade, and seeing someone else sitting under your palm tree. Israel had lost a portion of their inheritance through disobedience, leading to eighteen years of enslavement under King Eglon of Moab. Finally, however, they cried out to God. The sound of repentance resounded throughout Israel, and God responded. If you have not been properly aligned with God, like Israel you can make a new commitment to return to God's presence. When you do, God will hear and respond to you. Sound produces movement: When God heard the sound of repentance from Israel, He began to move. Heaven is waiting to move on your behalf. It is time for you to receive new war strategies so that you begin to possess your portion. Never forget that God has allotted you a portion. This is your inheritance, and you must possess your designated allotment in each season.

Israel's portion was being consumed by King Eglon in the form of an annual tribute. Imagine working hard every day only to have your resources hijacked by an enemy. You cannot make plans for your future because you know you will not have enough resources. Each year a representative was chosen to take the annual tribute to King Eglon; after eighteen years, this task fell to Ehud, a Benjamite. I am sure that this particular year, like the ones before, King Eglon awaited Israel's tribute with great expectation. He had bullied Israel for eighteen years; he had grown fat on the increase of Israel and expected to continue consuming the fruits of their labor.

This is a picture of the cycle of labor without rewards. When this cycle operates, you work each day earning a decent salary but somehow you never have enough. Perhaps you are the leader of a business or ministry and you have noticed that you are losing revenue from your business, but are unsure why. Or maybe unexpected doctor bills and other issues keep consuming your portion. These are just a couple of examples of how a robbing spirit operates. When your finances are biblically aligned, and you practice principles of good stewardship, you should increase. If you have not honored God in your finances, repentance will overcome this cycle. Take a moment and pray this simple prayer:

Lord, I thank You that You have given me the power to create wealth according to Deuteronomy 8:18. You have encoded my DNA to create wealth. I rebuke every robbing spirit that has been attacking my finances, health, peace or any other blessing that is due to me. I am increasing more and more. I will not lack any good thing. I decree that wealth, health, favor, overflowing portions and supersized blessings will mark my life from this day forward, in Jesus' name.

For King Eglon, he did not know what was coming. He did not know that Israel's return to God would become the catalyst for divine retribution to be released on Israel's behalf. He did not know that he was about to return their goods with interest. Now, because the sound of repentance and realignment with God was heard in Israel, God would bring an end to King Eglon's reign of terror. God was declaring, "Safe passage!" and initiating a cycle of restoration and retribution on Israel's behalf.

As a young girl in elementary school, I was bullied one year. At the end of every school day, this bully would come looking for me. I knew this, so every day I ran out of the school building and did not stop running until I was home. Even though we only lived three blocks from the school I attended, those three blocks felt like three miles.

One day as I was running home with the bully chasing me, I ran past my oldest brother, who caught me by the back of my jacket and asked, "Are you running from her?"

"Yes," I replied. "She is going to beat me up."

My brother's response was, "You are not running another day. Today, you are going to confront this situation. I'm here with you; it will be okay."

Several lessons can be gleaned from my childhood story:

- You will never overcome what you do not confront. You must recognize the seasons when you will need to face off with your enemy.
- God never sends you into battle without heaven's resources.
- The enemy distorts his size. He is never as large or powerful as he wants you to think, and he is *never* bigger than God!
- Even if you are afraid, confront your enemy. God will be there with you.

The end of the story is that only when I turned to face the bully could I see that she was not as large as I thought. Actually, she was smaller than I was. I was still afraid, but my brother standing and watching gave me confidence. Knowing that all of heaven is with you will help you to overcome fear. I once heard someone say, "Even if you are afraid, do it anyway. Do it afraid." Satan is a bully who will continue to steal your portion until you confront him.

In my dream about safe passage, I had been running and hiding from the enemy. All of a sudden, I had the feeling that it was time for a face-off. I decided to confront my enemy. When I made this decision, God was right there with me. No matter what the reason, if you are in a season of loss, God wants to change it. Certain sounds release heaven to move on your behalf. If you need to repent for unbelief, prayerlessness or some other issue, do not delay. Repent! Let the sound of repentance be released, and watch God respond.

APPLICATION

If there are areas of your life that are not submitted fully to the Lord, take a moment and repent. The sound of your repentance will release God to move on your behalf in a new way.

After repentance, it is time to recover your portion, which is your inheritance. What has been taken from you? What is being held up? What promises are timed for today or tomorrow that you are waiting to see manifested? Have you had enough? When you decide to confront the enemy that has held you captive in a season of loss, God will be there. God never sends us into battle alone. Heaven always goes with us. As an act of faith, I want you to shout, "Enough is enough! I have had enough!"

Once the enemy has occupied any part of your assigned portion, he never leaves voluntarily. You must throw him out! You must gain revelation from God regarding the war strategy that will displace the enemy from your assigned portion.

LAW OF REVELATION

Kingdom citizens must gain war strategies to overcome demonic powers.

Ehud was an unusual strategist and warrior; he was trained to fight with his left hand. This ability most likely confused his opponents since they did not know which hand he might use. He could switch in the middle of a confrontation. Ehud was not your average warrior! He also created a weapon that would destroy Israel's enemies. The war strategy he was tasked with executing involved him confronting Israel's enemy alone. So he prepared for himself the right weapon: "Ehud made himself a sword with two sharp edges that was about 12 inches long. He tied the sword to his right thigh and hid it under his uniform" (Judges 3:16 ERV). Notice that the sword was twelve inches long. This speaks to me because twelve is considered by many biblical interpreters to be a perfect number that symbolizes God's power and authority, as well as serving as a perfect governmental foundation. Not only that, but the sword symbolized the Word of God:

> God's word is alive and working and is sharper than a double-edged sword. It cuts all the way into us, where the soul and the spirit are joined, to the center of our joints and bones. And it judges the thoughts and feelings in our hearts.
>
> Hebrews 4:12 NCV

In effect, Ehud was armed with the Word of God. Hebrews 4:12 says the Word of God is sharper than the sharpest sword and cuts all the way into us. Ehud also attached the sword to his thigh, not his arm. Your thigh muscle connects your hips and knees and is essential to your mobility. Ehud's attachment of a twelve-inch, two-edged sword to his thigh was part of his war strategy. He was going to walk in God's Word—filled, as I see it, with the authority and power of God's government—to deliver a message to Israel's enemy: "It's time for retribution."

Victory Comes with Capacity

God always has a plan of victory for you. Revelation brings you into an understanding of God's plan, timing and way of execution. David prepared for his battle with Goliath when he worked for his father as a young shepherd. While working in the family business, David killed a lion and then a bear. His warrior capacity was expanding. Like David, sometimes you will find yourself in situations that God uses to expand your warrior capacity. Each confrontation increases you for future wars. Your trajectory will be sharp. Every confrontation with your enemy must be marked with a revelatory war strategy. Your battles will be different throughout the course of your life, and your war strategies must be obtained during times of prayer and worship. These are important keys to overthrowing demonic forces that come against you.

Ehud, a left-handed man, had been chosen sovereignly to deliver the annual tribute to King Eglon. You see, God had chosen Ehud to deliver an entire nation. We should notice that God could use Ehud because he had aligned himself with God, which placed Ehud in a position of achieving victory. Retribution can manifest for a family, a region or, in this case, an entire nation. Ehud knew enough was enough! Israel had been paying tribute for eighteen years, and it was time for the cycle to end.

The meaning of the number eighteen is linked with bondage. The Bible records the healing of a woman who had been bent over for eighteen years (Luke 13:11–13). Imagine that— her body was bent over, so that all she could see were people's feet. She could not stand erect or see the sky. She could not look someone in the eyes while holding a conversation. A demon of infirmity was keeping her bent over. Satan often operates in this way. He tries to keep you bent over in poverty, depression, unanswered prayers and many other means of oppression. If he is allowed to operate against us, we lose hope.

Jesus noticed the woman and called her to Himself. She was in the right place at the right time. I do not know if she got out of bed that day knowing that she was living her last day bent over. I believe she was going through that day as she had gone through all the previous ones. Eighteen years is a long time. Could it be that having been bent over so long, she had grown accustomed to her position? Could it be that she had no expectation that her situation would ever change? What is your situation? How long have you been bent over? This woman, whom Scripture does not name, did not ask for healing. She was positioned sovereignly for restoration and retribution. Her path was about to intersect the path of Jesus! She could have lived the rest of her life bent over, but she did not. She responded to the voice of the Lord. Not only did Jesus heal this woman, He also reconnected her with her inheritance, referring to her as "a daughter of Abraham" (Luke 13:16). That is retribution! That is how change is initiated. What you are unwilling to confront will never change.

> ## APPLICATION
>
> Change is initiated through confrontation. What you are unwilling to confront will never change. The status quo will continue until you confront whatever is blocking your blessings.

Ehud was ready to confront the enemy, King Eglon of Moab, and bring an end to Israel's cycle of loss. Ehud did not just have a good idea; he had received a prophetic war strategy from God. He decided to go back and bring an end to their season of loss. Your season of loss will change when you decide that you have had enough. Ehud was a judge in the tribe of Benjamin and was chosen by God to pass judgment on King Eglon and his cohorts. Are you ready for change? God wants you to pass judgment on your situation.

After delivering the tribute, Ehud and his men left. I believe King Eglon was in a celebratory mood because he had just received his annual offering from Israel. Ehud returned and told Eglon he had a message for him that was to be delivered privately. Could it be that King Eglon's mood created a false hope that Ehud had more to give him? Rather than receiving an additional tribute, King Eglon was pierced through with the sword Ehud carried under his garment, strapped to his thigh. Wow! Ehud plunged his knife into Eglon so deep into his fat belly that the handle broke off in his stomach and the tip of the sword came out through his back with fat on it. This double-edged sword was twelve inches long. Eglon was not a small man; he was obese. This means that Ehud's hand and forearm went into Eglon. That is deep! Confrontation carries a measure of strength. Ehud would need strength to plunge his sword deep enough into Eglon to break the handle inside of him and push the sword out through his back. When you are in position to confront your enemies, a supernatural spirit of confrontation comes upon you, giving you strength to over-come your enemies. Poverty and continued loss weaken you. Weak prayers laced with unbelief do not bring you through your seasons of restoration and retribution. You must be armed in the might of God to overcome your enemies. Remember, all of heaven wars with you.

APPLICATION

What have you avoided confronting that is robbing your portion? Some people mistakenly believe that if they stay away from the dimension of spiritual warfare, their lives will be better. Remember, what you refuse to confront will never change.

God is strong, and he wants you strong. So take everything the Master has set out for you, well-made weapons of the best materials. And put them to use so you will be able to stand up to everything the Devil throws your way. This is no afternoon athletic contest that we'll walk away from and forget about in a couple of hours. This is for keeps, a life-or-death fight to the finish against the Devil and all his angels.

Ephesians 6:10–12 MESSAGE

The Bible describes a tribute as a present, a mark of respect. While Israel was crying out to the Lord and preparing their present, Ehud was making a sword. Ehud knew that something had to change. Could it be that the cry of Israel's misery had become overwhelming to Ehud, and he knew that it was time for a confrontation? After presenting King Eglon with Israel's gift, as he left, Ehud and his men passed the sculptured stones at Gilgal. That was the turning point. We should understand that in every season of restoration and retribution there comes a moment of turning, or a tipping point. It is that moment when the synergy of change overtakes the current cycle and unleashes the new. Could it be possible that Ehud was stirred to action by the memorial stone at Gilgal symbolizing Israel's past victories?

The stones at Gilgal had been placed after God supernaturally withheld the waters of the Jordan so that Israel could cross over into the Promised Land (see Joshua 4:19–24); they served as a demonstration that God was alive and well. God wants it known and wants it to be remembered that He is a living God who acts on behalf of His people. The stones served as a memorial to the living God.

Gilgal was so named because it means the "rolling" or "to roll away." God was saying, "I have rolled away the past. I have rolled away the reproach of Egypt, and I separated you from all those taunts against you that you would never get into the Promised Land." These stones were a reminder that they were now a separated people—separated from the past, but also separated unto a living God. It is what circumcision is all about. It was a sign that they had made a covenant with God.

135

Gilgal symbolically stands for separation: being separated from the past and separated unto God. This is a powerful reminder. In a culture that seems intent on removing God from public places and spaces, you might be tempted to shift into a place of compromise. God wants you to remember His goodness expressed toward you and your family in past seasons. I encourage you to keep a memorial or testimony journal to chronicle the great things God has done and is continuing to do for you. When the enemy tries to overtake you with unbelief, go back and read your history with the Lord and let faith arise again.

Secret Kills

Ehud left his men and went back to King Eglon's private chamber to confront his nation's enemy. Back in the king's presence, Ehud told him, "I have a secret message for you, O king. . . . I have a message from God for you" (Judges 3:19–20 AMP). King Eglon sent everyone from the room and stood up to hear the message. *The time is for restoration! Retribution has come!*— that was God's message. Ehud confronted the enemy, killed him, locked the door and left. That is what I call a "secret kill." He did not raise a victory roar; he quietly went out the back door. God gave Ehud safe passage. He walked right past his enemies! There will be some battles that you will not be able to share with everyone. God will give you strategies that will be executed quietly, but they will be effective. There are times when the strategy from heaven requires a team to stand and war with you, and there are times when God's strategy sends you on a secret kill to dismantle the structure of the enemy. The team will pray for you as you go. It is important to know God's strategy for every season of war.

Ehud did not stop at killing King Eglon. Restoration was not enough; it was time for retribution. It was time for Israel's divine payback. Israel was going to receive more than they had lost. When he was far enough from the king's house, Ehud blew the trumpet, and Israel assembled. That day, led by Ehud, Israel pursued King Eglon's army, killing approximately ten thousand Moabite soldiers. The Bible describes the Moabite soldiers as well fed and robust (see Judges 3:29 MESSAGE). They were not weak or scrawny. But Israel was not deterred by their size, for they were in a supernatural moment. It is not enough to defeat one demon; you must use God's war strategy to dismantle the entire confederacy operating against you in every season. Israel ran their enemies out of the land. This can only be done through Kingdom revelation. Take a moment and identify today any area of your inheritance the enemy is occupying. It is time to believe God for a new war strategy to run your enemies out of town! Do not let the enemy occupy your inheritance as demonic squatters. Run them off! David overlooked the size of Goliath and defeated him with a sling shot. Ignore the size of your enemies; look at the size of God. Find time each day to decree and pray these prayers over your life:

I dismantle every threefold cord of wickedness that has been set against me. I rebuke the spirit of the Amalekite, Ammonite and Moabite that comes to plunder me and steal my inheritance. I remind you that the blood of Christ is in my blood, and a bloodline has been set around my stuff.

I have the authority to dismantle you and forbid you to operate. I say, "Stop! In Jesus' name."

I dismantle every satanic calendar, every anniversary demon that operates in my life. The cycle is broken today, in Jesus' name.

As heaven wars with me, I overcome every assignment of labor without reward, which is poverty, in Jesus' name.

||||||||||||||||||||||||||||||||||||||||||||||||||||||||||||||||||||||||||||||||||||||||||||||||

Key Scriptures: Judges 3:16; Deuteronomy 25:17–19; 1 Samuel 15:2–3; Ephesians 6:10–12

Key Points:

- Restoration is reestablishment or bringing back into existence, while retribution is exacting punishment on our enemies for taking our inheritance or delaying our blessings in the first place.

- Retribution is the spoils of war that belong to the believers and should not be left on the battlefield.

- Avoid trying to war through human wisdom; it is only through Kingdom revelation that you gain war strategies to defeat your enemies.

- God always has a plan of victory for you. Revelation brings you into an understanding of God's plan, timing and way of execution.

- Change is initiated through confrontation. What you are unwilling to confront will never change. The status quo will continue until you confront whatever is blocking your blessings.

- Some people mistakenly believe that if they stay away from the dimension of spiritual warfare, their lives will be better.

- Law of revelation: Kingdom citizens must gain war strategies to overcome demonic powers.

Reflection: Is any of your portion being stolen by the enemy? Make a list of what has been stolen and ask the Lord to give you a war strategy to overthrow your enemy who is holding your portion.

_____

_____

_____

_____

_____

_____

CHAPTER TEN

Armed and Dangerous

For though we walk in the flesh [as mortal men], we are not carrying on our [spiritual] warfare according to the flesh and using the weapons of man. The weapons of our warfare are not physical [weapons of flesh and blood]. Our weapons are divinely powerful for the destruction of fortresses. We are destroying sophisticated arguments and every exalted and proud thing that sets itself up against the [true] knowledge of God, and we are taking every thought and purpose captive to the obedience of Christ.

2 Corinthians 10:3–5 AMP

Currently in America, it is rare to watch the nightly news without hearing at least one report of someone who engaged in violent criminal activity and is described in the newscast as "armed and dangerous." In such situations, other branches of law enforcement beyond the local police force usually mobilize—in some cases, SWAT teams are activated to facilitate the individual's capture. These teams do not go in unequipped; not only are they sent to seize the individual armed, they have access to an arsenal far larger than what is available to most individuals. I use this picture to show how we, as Kingdom citizens, have been spiritually armed. Demonic forces would like you to believe that you are defenseless against them. Do not believe the lie! You are armed to overcome your enemy. You have access to the arsenal of heaven. God deploys His angel armies on your behalf. When you stand in faith, believing God's Word over the lies of hell, you become dangerous to every assignment of hell set against you.

The apostle Paul instructs us concerning the "weapons of our warfare." We are not contending against flesh and blood. Our warfare is against powerful forces of hell committed to our failure. It is the goal of hell to block responses to your prayers by overwhelming you with ideas and ways of thinking that weaken your faith. Using military language, Paul wanted believers to understand their identity as Kingdom warriors who have access to the arsenal of heaven. Our military campaign is not finished until we have overcome every enemy opposing us in that season. We are anointed to defeat every argument and all human reasoning designed to weaken our faith. God did not send us into battle against our enemy alone. We are heavily armed soldiers!

> Put on the full armor of God [for His precepts are like the splendid armor of a heavily-armed soldier], so that you may be able to [successfully] stand up against all the schemes and the strategies and the deceits of the devil. For our struggle is not against flesh and blood [contending only with physical opponents], but against the rulers, against the powers, against the world forces of this [present] darkness, against the spiritual forces of wickedness in the heavenly (supernatural) places.
>
> Ephesians 6:11–12 AMP

The weaponry we have operates through faith and is more than capable of demolishing demonic powers attempting to

141

hinder our prayers. Another way to view our weaponry is as battle gear. Each day, we must be fully dressed in the armor of God so that we overcome our enemies. Our battle against our enemy is spiritual. Although we see the outcomes in the natural realm, we are not fighting against a flesh and blood enemy. It takes spiritual weapons given to us by God to overcome.

Weapon #1: Our Kingdom Authority

Kingdom identity is linked with Kingdom authority. Understanding the concept of the Kingdom is a vital key in understanding your authority as a Kingdom citizen. Too many believers lack understanding in this area and, as a result, are unable to walk in the full measure of authority of their Kingdom citizenship. As citizens of the Kingdom of God, we have power and authority to rule on earth.

God, the rightful owner of earth, chose to give earth to man to manage and steward, as Psalm 115:16 (NIV1984) states: "The highest heavens belong to the LORD, but the earth he has given to man." As the creator of the universe, God has the sovereign right to give earth to mankind to rule and steward.

> In the beginning [before all time] was the Word (Christ), and the Word was with God, and the Word was God Himself. He was [continually existing] in the beginning [co-eternally] with God. All things were made and came into existence through Him; and without Him not even one thing was made that has come into being.
>
> John 1:1–3 AMP

When Jesus came to earth, He came as Redeemer, and He also came as King. A study of Jesus' ministry on earth shows that He preached and demonstrated the power of the Kingdom of God. In other words, Jesus announced the arrival and reestablishment of the Kingdom, which is something only a king could do. As King, Jesus is automatically Lord. As Myles Munroe writes,

> The Lordship of Jesus is by creative rights and was a natural result of His role in the Creation of all things, both seen and unseen. In essence, we do not "make" Jesus Lord; He is Lord by creative right, whether we acknowledge Him or not.[1]

A distinguishing characteristic of Jesus' ministry was authority. The word *authority* is a translation of the Greek word *exousia*, which means power. *Strong's Concordance* describes *exousia* as the power of authority (influence) and right (privilege)[2]; it is the power of rule or government, belonging to Him whose will and commands must be submitted to by others and obeyed.[3] This is exactly what we see in Jesus' ministry:

> And they were astonished at His doctrine, for He taught them as one who had authority, and not as the scribes.
>
> Mark 1:22

> And they were all amazed, insomuch that they questioned among themselves, saying, "What thing is this? What new doctrine is this? For with authority he commandeth even the unclean spirits, and they obey him."
>
> Mark 1:27

Jesus not only walked in authority, He gave authority to His disciples. You cannot give away authority unless you are operating in a greater measure of authority. Jesus was both Lord and King, giving Him authority to delegate authority.[4]

> "My kingdom is not of this world [nor does it have its origin in this world]. If My kingdom were of this world, My servants

143

would be fighting [hard] to keep Me from being handed over to the Jews; but as it is, My kingdom is not of this world."

So Pilate said to Him, "Then You are a King?"

Jesus answered, "You say [correctly] that I am a King. This is why I was born, and for this I have come into the world, to testify to the truth."

John 18:36–37 AMP

Then He called His twelve disciples together, and gave them power and authority over all devils and to cure diseases. And He sent them to preach the Kingdom of God and to heal the sick.

Luke 9:1–2

After these things the Lord appointed seventy others also, and sent them two by two ahead of Him into every city and place whither He Himself would come. . . . "Heal the sick that are therein and say unto them, 'The Kingdom of God is come nigh unto you.'"

Luke 10:1, 9

The same authority that was given to His disciples has been given to us. One reason we do not operate in the measure of authority given to us is because we do not understand the Kingdom of God. Too often we confuse the Kingdom with denominationalism. But Jesus did not come to establish a denomination, He came to establish His Kingdom. "Receive this truth: Whatever you forbid on earth will be considered to be forbidden in heaven, and whatever you release on earth will be considered to be released in heaven" (Matthew 18:18 TPT).

God created man to rule the earth. Adam and Eve were placed in the Garden of Eden and were given authority to rule over everything that had been created. When Adam and Eve sinned, rulership of the earth was handed over to Satan. When Jesus came, rulership was reinstated to Kingdom citizens. As a Kingdom citizen, you have been endowed by God with authority of rulership on earth, and anything opposing you is illegal. This means that when answers to your prayers are delayed, it is an illegal operation of the kingdom of darkness.

> God created man in His own image, in the image of God created He him; male and female created He them. And God blessed them, and God said unto them, "Be fruitful and multiply, and replenish the earth, and subdue it; and have dominion over the fish of the sea, and over the fowl of the air, and over every living thing that moveth upon the earth."
>
> Genesis 1:27–28

The dominion man was given placed him in charge of the earth. Man ruled over every living thing. Adam assigned names to everything God created. He was a ruler of a territory with a female counterpart capable of helping him to rule. Adam was a king and Eve a queen. God, as supreme King of the universe, possesses authority to give kingship to mankind. We are God's delegated rulers on the earth.

> But you are God's chosen treasure—priests who are kings, a spiritual "nation" set apart as God's devoted ones. He called you out of darkness to experience his marvelous light, and now he claims you as his very own. He did this so that you would broadcast his glorious wonders throughout the world.
>
> 1 Peter 2:9 TPT

> From Jesus Christ the Faithful Witness, the Firstborn from among the dead and the ruling King, who rules over the kings of the earth! Now to the one who constantly loves us and has loosed us from our sins by his own blood, and to the one who has made us to rule as a kingly priesthood to serve his God and Father—to him be glory and dominion throughout the eternity of eternities! Amen!
>
> Revelation 1:5–6 TPT

Weapon #2: The Word of God

The Word of God helps us to overcome ignorance. The Word of God also helps us to know God's will and contains revelatory keys to overcoming our enemy. Hell does not have authority over you. You have been endowed with Kingdom right and might! The only way hell can overcome you is if you stop fighting. We have been given the right of rulership on the earth. We were given keys of the Kingdom. Many believers mistakenly interpret this to mean, "keys *to* the Kingdom." As Kingdom citizens, we were given keys *of* the Kingdom, meaning we have been given keys that will unlock the power of the Kingdom in our lives. These keys are found in the Word of God. Myles Munroe writes,

> We who are Kingdom citizens are supposed to be operating on a level that blows other people's minds. We should have access to a power that mystifies those who are not yet in the Kingdom. We are supposed to be living life at a certain level where we are tapping into resources that others cannot explain.[5]

The keys we have been given are knowledge. We have the capacity to understand how the Kingdom of God operates. This is why it is important to overcome ignorance. If you are operating in ignorance, you will not see more of your prayers answered. The powers of darkness will use your ignorance and lack of knowledge against you.

Weapon #3: The Name of Jesus

The key that opens the resources of heaven is prayer in the name of Jesus. When Kingdom citizens pray in faith, aligning with God's Word, our heavenly Father responds. Too often we pray in Jesus' name as though it were some magical formula. We do not pray from our position as Kingdom citizens who operate in delegated authority. If you were given someone's power of attorney, you have full rights and privileges to transact business in that person's name. When you use that name, it is as though the person who has given you his or her authority—the power of attorney—were actually present. Whatever business you are transacting in that moment must be completed. It is the same when we pray in Jesus' name. As Kingdom citizens, we have been given full rights of kingship on earth. Hell must submit when we stand in our authority. Maybe you have been waiting for responses for months or even years. Daniel waited 21 days; Abram and Sarai waited more than twenty years. Keep asking, keep seeking and keep knocking—a response is coming. When we ask according to God's will and His purposes, heaven will respond.

Myles Munroe writes that keys represent seven dimensions: authority, access, ownership, control, authorization, power and freedom.[6] All of those words indicate a high degree of influence! Have you ever considered how unfair it would be for God to assign you a destiny and a portion on earth, knowing there was an enemy trying to keep you from your portion, and not give you the weapons to overcome him? That is not who God is. As citizens of the Kingdom of God, we have access to every weapon we need to overcome our enemy.

Weapon #4: Heaven's Armies

Angels are a part of heaven's army. Our eyes must be opened to see how angels are working with us, as they were for the servant of the man of God. He got up early and went out to find an army with horses and chariots encircling the city:

> Elisha's servant said to him, "Oh no, my master! What are we to do?"

147

Elisha answered, "Do not be afraid, for those who are with us are more than those who are with them." Then Elisha prayed and said, "Lord, please, open his eyes that he may see."

And the Lord opened the servant's eyes and he saw; and behold, the mountain was full of horses and chariots of fire surrounding Elisha. When the Arameans came down to him, Elisha prayed to the Lord and said, "Please strike this people (nation) with blindness." And God struck them with blindness, in accordance with Elisha's request.

2 Kings 6:15–18 AMP

The Body of Christ is becoming more aware of how heaven is present with us on earth. When I was a child, I would sometimes refer to my guardian angel; in my mind, this was an angel sent by God to protect me. I did not understand how vast God's host of angels was, and I certainly did not understand how the angels fight on our behalf. It is clear from Scripture that they do. For example, when Daniel prayed and waited three weeks for a response, an angel appeared on the 21st day to explain that Daniel's prayers had been answered on the first day. A ruling spirit, the prince of Persia, was attempting to hold back the angel who had been dispatched with Daniel's response. In order to overcome the ruling power, war was necessary. Michael, one of the war angels, was mobilized for this purpose and prevailed. In the passage from 2 Kings, the eyes of Elisha's servant were opened to see the host of heaven's army positioned to fight on their behalf. Our eyes must be opened to "see" how the angels are working around us.

Not all angels have a warring function. I was speaking to a friend who shared a dream of an angel. She described him as being larger than the room and very muscular, and when she looked at his face, written on his forehead was the word *strength*. She then understood the angel had come to give strength during a crisis she and others were experiencing at that time.

My first encounter with an angel was during a praise and worship moment in a corporate gathering. As I worshiped, I heard the Spirit of God say, *Look at the altar area in front of the church.* When I looked, I saw an angel who appeared to be more than nine feet tall, and his wings, folded close to his body, were as tall as he was. He was arrayed in white—not an ordinary white; his garment appeared to be luminescent, glowing. In fact, I could see through him; he appeared to be three-dimensional. The room was filled with the glory of the Lord. The *Shekinah* presence of the Lord permeated the room.[7] That day, angels radiating with the glory of the Lord filled the worship service.

> Then I looked, and I heard the voices of myriads of angels in circles around the throne, as well as the voices of the living creatures and the elders—myriads and myriads!
>
> Revelation 5:11 TPT

> And God has never said this to any of his angels: "Take your seat next to me at my right hand until I force your whispering enemies to be a rug under your feet." What role then, do the angels have? The angels are spirit-messengers sent by God to serve those who are going to be saved.
>
> Hebrews 1:13–14 TPT

We do not worship angels. God releases angelic help to assist in our Kingdom destiny. There are more angels than you or I can count; that is what the word *myriad* means: countless. You and I have access to countless angels to help us to overcome every obstacle. The issue is not whether heaven *can* help us. The issue is whether we will ask and believe that heaven *will* help us.

Weapon #5: Revelation

We have previously discussed the importance of revelation as the source of our war strategy. We war from a position of revelation. In every war season, we must gain revelatory strategies to overcome our enemies. God's Word not only contains promises to us but the keys of the Kingdom. The enemy will put a stronghold next to your gift to prevent you from seeing more of your prayers answered. This stronghold attempts to cover your gift so that you cannot see how to move forward. This is why we need revelation.

> You have been given a teachable heart to perceive the secret, hidden mysteries of God's kingdom realm. But to those who don't have a listening heart, my words are merely stories. Even though they have eyes, they are blind to the true meaning of what I say, and even though they listen, they won't receive full revelation.
>
> Luke 8:10 TPT

Weapon #6: Prophecy and Prophetic Decrees

Prophecy is an inspired utterance from God, which He uses to make known His will and release revelatory strategies and instructions. When prophecy is released, God is speaking out of the timeless place where He dwells into time. Prophecy and psychic readings do not originate from the same source. Prophecy occurs when God reveals His intentions for an individual, a region or nations through a Kingdom citizen. Psychic readings come through the kingdom of darkness and should not be used as a source of information. When God speaks, He fulfills His Word! "For I am [actively] watching over My word to fulfill it" (Jeremiah 1:12 AMP).

> For as the rain and snow come down from heaven, and do not return there without watering the earth, making it bear and

sprout, and providing seed to the sower and bread to the eater, so will My word be which goes out of My mouth; it will not return to Me void (useless, without result), without accomplishing what I desire, and without succeeding in the matter for which I sent it.

Isaiah 55:10–11 AMP

Prophetic declarations are another dimension of prophecy. Just as in times of prayer we pray the Scriptures, prophetic declarations are inspired utterances that make known the will and intentions of God in a particular situation. Declarations are prophetic statements that release faith in us, helping us to look beyond our current circumstances and see how heaven is moving on our behalf. Prophetic declarations are connected to the law of language creativity. "You will also decide and decree a thing, and it will be established for you; and the light [of God's favor] will shine upon your ways" (Job 22:28 AMP).

Weapon # 7: Discernment

Discernment is God's ability working in us to see beyond natural facts. We were created with spiritual capacity, which means that we can perceive spiritual things. We do not, however, always know what we are perceiving. You might have only a sense that something does not seem right and later find out that something has indeed gone wrong. Several years ago, my late husband and I returned home from an evening worship gathering. As we arrived at our driveway, we both had a sense that something was wrong. We had not entered our house, but we had a knowing feeling that something was not right inside.

Instead of opening the garage door as he normally did, my husband parked across the street. We were not expecting what we found. At first glance, our house appeared just as we had left it, but a closer inspection revealed the lock on the front door had been broken. We immediately contacted the police, who determined that our house had been broken into. Because of the gift of discernment, my husband sensed a problem before having actual proof that a burglar had been in our home. That is an example of discernment in action: supernatural capacity given to us by God to see beyond natural facts. Discernment is a revelatory gift of the Spirit that can help you as you press forward to seeing your prayers answered.

Weapon #8: Fasting

As a young believer in Christ, I developed a pattern of fasting and prayer. I quickly noticed how fasting became an accelerant to my prayers. Stubborn issues that seemed to be persistent were broken when I included fasting. I remember reading books written by many of the well-known faith healers and evangelists from an earlier era. The more I read about their experiences, the more encouraged I was to find time for fasting. It was very helpful to me that the church I had joined planned regular times for corporate water fasts. Fasting is a weapon that can help you to overcome stubborn issues blocking your faith. Fasting also helps to unblock your spiritual channels, allowing you to become more sensitive to receiving revelation. A study of the book of Daniel reveals Daniel fasting on several occasions when he was waiting for a response to his prayers.

> I, Daniel, understood from the books the number of years which, according to the word of the LORD to Jeremiah the prophet, must pass before the desolations [which had been] pronounced on Jerusalem would end; and it was seventy years. So I directed my attention to the Lord God to seek Him by prayer and supplications, with fasting, sackcloth and ashes. I prayed to the LORD my God and confessed and said . . . "Now

therefore, our God, listen to (heed) the prayer of Your servant (Daniel) and his supplications."

Daniel 9:2–4, 17 AMP

While studying Israel's history, Daniel recognized that the season of God's judgment spoken to Jeremiah had ended. Seventy years of judgment had passed, and now it was time for Israel's restoration. Daniel's response was to *direct* his attention to the Lord God, to seek Him by prayer and supplications, with fasting, sackcloth and ashes.

> While I was still speaking and praying, and confessing my sin and the sin of my people Israel, and presenting my supplication before the LORD my God in behalf of the holy mountain of my God, while I was still speaking in prayer and extremely exhausted, the man Gabriel, whom I had seen in the earlier vision, came to me about the time of the evening sacrifice. He instructed me and he talked with me and said, "O Daniel, I have now come to give you insight and wisdom and understanding. At the beginning of your supplications, the command [to give you an answer] was issued, and I have come to tell you, for you are highly regarded and greatly beloved."

Daniel 9:20–23 AMP

Daniel pressed beyond the weakness of his body and reached the point of still speaking in prayer though extremely exhausted. You may experience fatigue during times of fasting and prayer, but do not give up. Keep pressing forward.

APPLICATION

You might not have capacity to fast 21 days like Daniel or 40 days like Jesus. Ask the Spirit of God to show you how you can fast. There are numerous books available that can help you understand the weapon of fasting and how to use it properly.

Weapon #9: Praise and Worship

Our praise is a weapon that overcomes the attacks of the enemy. When you are under attack, the first area where the enemy will try to overcome you is praise and worship. Satan knows the power of your praise, and he seeks to discourage and frustrate you into silence.

> Break forth with dancing! Make music and sing God's praises with the rhythm of drums! For he enjoys his faithful lovers. He adorns the humble with his beauty and he loves to give them the victory. His godly lovers triumph in the glory of God, and their joyful praises will rise even while others sleep.
> God's high and holy praises fill their mouths, for their shouted praises are their weapons of war! These warring weapons will bring vengeance on every opposing force and every resistant power—to bind kings with chains and rulers with iron shackles. Praise-filled warriors will enforce the judgment-doom decreed against their enemies. This is the glorious honor he gives to all his godly lovers.
>
> Psalm 149:3–9 TPT

Key Scriptures: 2 Corinthians 10:3–5; Ephesians 6:11–12; John 1:1–3; Matthew 18:18; Isaiah 55:10–11; Daniel 9; Psalm 149

Key Points: We have been given supernatural weapons of warfare.
- Weapon #1: Our Kingdom authority. Our Kingdom identity and authority are linked. What is released in heaven is also released on earth.

154

- Weapon #2: The Word of God. The Word of God helps us to overcome ignorance and to know God's will.
- Weapon #3: The name of Jesus. When Kingdom citizens pray in the name of Jesus, in alignment with God's Word, our heavenly Father responds.
- Weapon #4: Heaven's armies. Angels are part of heaven's army. Our eyes must be opened to see how angels are working around us.
- Weapon #5: Revelation. We war from a position of Kingdom revelation.
- Weapon #6: Prophecy and prophetic decrees. Prophecy is inspired utterance from God which He uses to make known His will and release revelatory strategies and instructions.
- Weapon #7: Discernment. Discernment is supernatural capacity given to us by God to see beyond natural facts.
- Weapon #8: Fasting. Fasting is a weapon that can help you to overcome stubborn sin issues and can also unblock your spiritual channels, allowing you to hear God's voice more clearly.
- Weapon #9: Praise and worship. Our praise is a weapon that overcomes the enemy.

Reflection: Review the nine weapons listed in this chapter. Which weapons are you most proficient in using? Ask the Lord to help you to increase your capacity and skill in using the weapons you are not as proficient with.

CHAPTER ELEVEN

Change the Game!

God is not a man, that He should lie, nor a son of man, that He should repent. Has He said, and will He not do it? Or has He spoken and will He not make it good and fulfill it?

Numbers 23:19 AMP

One evening I was observing my nieces and nephew playing a game of cards. I was not observing them in a way they could detect; rather, I was observing through listening. Young children are interesting to observe, especially when they are at play in a rules-based game. Most adults simply read the instructions and play the game according to the rules. That is not what young children do. Young children tend to change the rules of the game to secure the win. The older sibling is often the victor. My nieces and nephew changed the rules each time they faced off with a new opponent younger than themselves. That is what you will need to do if you are going to see more of your prayers answered. The way you prayed in your last season will need to change in your new season. Once you develop an immunity to an attack the enemy has brought against you time and time again, he will change his way of operating against you. The devil is going to be the devil, but the way he comes against you can change. In every war season, you must access heaven's war strategies to overcome your enemy. Heaven's war strategies for you will change in each season of war. God will fulfill His promises to you.

War Strategies

In ancient wars, many cities were fortified behind a wall with a tower called a stronghold. The stronghold was a vantage point and was difficult to penetrate. From here significant attacks could be launched. To overcome these obstacles, a successful war strategy needed to be developed. Not until the stronghold could be penetrated could the attacking forces hope to gain the greater advantage. As previously stated, the enemy will attempt to establish a stronghold next to your gift to prevent your gift from operating.

This reminds me of the childhood fairy tale "Rapunzel," about a princess who had been locked in a tower without stairs or doors. The only way in or out was a high window. In order for anyone to get inside the tower, Princess Rapunzel had to let down her extremely long hair so the person could climb it; thus her hair became an access point. In war, the stronghold is used to keep invading forces out—when the stronghold has been penetrated, it can be used to let invading forces in. Any stronghold that the enemy has tried to establish next to your gift can and must be overturned. Gaining war strategies from heaven will help you to pull down demonic strongholds and uncover your gift. This is how you change the game. There is no greater strategist than Lord Sabaoth, the Man of war.

We can see this war principle of changing the game when Israel emerged from the wilderness. God's strategy for Israel to conquer Jericho was a walk around the city once a day for six days, and then seven times while shouting on the seventh day. In the book of Judges, each of the judges God raised up as a deliverer for Israel was given a different war strategy to overcome his enemies. Ehud, the left-handed warrior, hid a twelve-inch knife beneath his garment. Without rallying the men of Israel against King Eglon, who had held Israel in captivity for eighteen years, Ehud met the king in his private chambers and performed a secret kill, thrusting his blade so deep that the tip came out through the king's back. When you are confronting your enemy, your annihilation must be thorough. You must totally cast down the demonic structure working against you. When he finished performing the secret kill, Ehud walked right past the king's men; only then did he mobilize the men of Israel.

An account of two of King David's battles against the Philistines is given in 1 Chronicles 14. In the first battle, God commanded King David to attack his enemies, so King David marched forward to confront the Philistines. After the victory King David said, "God hath broken in upon mine enemies by mine hand like the breaking forth of waters" (1 Chronicles 14:11). The next time King David faced the same enemy, God changed the game, instructing King David to come at his enemies from the opposite direction. King David's signal was a sound going over the tops of the mulberry trees. My point here is to encourage you to get a revelatory war strategy from God. The key to your victory will be to receive and execute the war strategy God gives you and to not quit until you see manifestation! Be willing to change the game as God directs you.

APPLICATION

Ask the Lord to show you how the enemy has been operating against you to steal your portion. As the Lord begins to

show you the enemy's tactics, let the Lord give you a war
strategy to overcome him.

Be Specific

Your diligent pursuit of seeing more answers to your prayers
will be rewarded. God delights in answering our prayers. Be
specific about what you are asking for. I often counsel individuals who want to get married to be specific about the kind
of spouse they want. I even encourage them to list their deal
breakers, those characteristics in another person they do not
feel they can live with. My point in doing this is to help them
pray more specifically. I encourage leaders to write out their vision and develop a needs list. What do you need to fulfill God's
purposes? What has not been released? Where there is vision,
there must be provision. Do not be vague. God is omniscient,
meaning He knows everything and cannot increase in knowledge. The details are to our advantage. Details help us to tap
into the heart and mind of God for our needs.

APPLICATION

Where are you being delayed? What portion have you yet to
see released? Write it down and take it daily before the Lord.

Don't bargain with God. Be direct. Ask for what you need. This
isn't a cat-and-mouse, hide-and-seek game we're in. If your
child asks for bread, do you trick him with sawdust? If he asks
for fish, do you scare him with a live snake on his plate? As bad
as you are, you wouldn't think of such a thing. You're at least
decent to your own children. So don't you think the God who
conceived you in love will be even better?

Matthew 7:7 MESSAGE

Persistence

I have watched runners in a marathon, and I have seen them becoming fatigued as they proceed along the course. When this happens, their pace often slows down. They do not seem to have the same level of energy. I heard a testimony of a minister who decided to run a 25-mile marathon. He had never run a marathon before, and to prepare himself, he committed to a rigorous training schedule. On the day of the race, when the starting signal sounded, he, along with hundreds of other runners, began running. He was feeling pretty good for the first fifteen miles. As he approached the eighteenth mile, he began feeling more and more tired. It was around this time that he experienced what is called "hitting the wall." Hitting the wall refers to depletion of glycogen stores while performing endurance exercise. It is a feeling athletes get when they "run out of steam" or "bonk out." The pastor's feet felt heavier with each step. Finally, when he thought he would quit, he noticed someone on the sidelines mouthing the words, "Don't quit." He finished the race.

At some point in your wait, you will be tempted to walk away from prayer, feeling as though it is not God's will. Persistence will be a vital key to resisting the assignments of hell trying to overcome you. When assignments of discouragement, frustration and vexation attempt to overwhelm you, it is time to change the game and get a new strategy from heaven.

Do Not Die in Your Wilderness

Pressing in to see more of your prayers answered can feel like being in the wilderness, the place "between." You are not where you were, but you have not arrived at your destination. The wilderness is designed to be a place of preparation, not a permanent dwelling place. In the wilderness, the enemy seeks to take advantage of what appears to be a moment of weakness.

I say it appears that way because you never stop having access to heaven's resources. Rather than give in to the temptations presented by the enemy, change the game. This involves gaining new revelatory strategies that will shift you forward.

> Then was Jesus led up by the Spirit into the wilderness to be tempted by the devil. And when He had fasted forty days and forty nights, He afterward hungered. . . . Then the devil left Him, and behold, angels came and ministered unto Him.
>
> Matthew 4:1–2, 11

Prior to beginning His ministry, Jesus spent forty days and nights fasting. From this passage we can learn several important principles that will help us gain the victory over our enemies:

1. Be led by Holy Spirit. Jesus' decision to enter the wilderness was not arbitrary; He was led by Holy Spirit. Seeing more of your prayers answered will require you to be led by Holy Spirit through your wilderness and into your season of manifestation.

2. Gain understanding of your seasons. Jesus knew He would face temptation from the enemy. Your wilderness has a purpose. It is important to know that you will encounter a wilderness face-off against your enemy. Gaining understanding of why the face-off has come will be helpful to your endurance.

3. There is a time to emerge from the wilderness. Jesus was in the wilderness for forty days. Moses was in the desert for forty years. The number forty symbolizes time; it refers to a season of testing and trials. It is important to remember that seasons end. Your wilderness season was never meant to last a lifetime.

4. The enemy will attack you in areas where you seem to be weak. He waited until Jesus was hungry. What are you

hungry for? Guard your appetites, especially during your wilderness season.

5. Secure your identity. The enemy attempted to influence Jesus to prove His identity as the Son of God by obeying demonically inspired commands. Satan wanted Jesus to provide for His own needs instead of waiting for heaven's provision. Do not react to the taunts of the enemy. Be secure in your Kingdom identity and trust God to provide for you.

6. Know your worth. The enemy will attempt to influence you to question your value to God. Do not leap off the mountain, leap on! Praise God in your wilderness.

7. Reject the lie. Satan wants you to believe that everything belongs to him. That is a lie! "The earth is the LORD's, and the fullness thereof, the world and they that dwell therein" (Psalm 24:1). Everything Satan was offering Jesus was already His! Your portion is coming—do not give up!

At the end of the temptation, heaven opened. The angels came and ministered to Jesus. You are never alone in your wilderness. Angels are there in ways you may not comprehend, waiting to strengthen you. Be persistent and do not give up. Restoration and retribution are going to be released in your life, family, ministry, business, etc.

A New Plumb Line

We are living in a season when God is resetting the plumb line among His people. According to the *Dictionary of Bible Themes*, a plumb line is

> a cord weighted with lead that is used in building to check that vertical structures are true. It is used symbolically to refer to the divine standard against which God, the builder of his people,

tests and judges them. It also symbolizes the standards by which God will rebuild his people.[1]

When Joel prophesied that God would restore, he was declaring a time when God would make His people whole again. "And I will compensate you for the years that the swarming locust has eaten, the creeping locust, the stripping locust, and the gnawing locust—My great army which I sent among you" (Joel 2:25 AMP). In that time of restoration God would bring to an end a season of judgment, opening the way for repayment for Israel's losses. The word *restore* includes the idea of retribution.[2]

Restoration has a set time; this is why you must gain an understanding of how God moves in time to bring forth everything He has promised for you. On the day of Pentecost, Peter announced the beginning of a season of restoration.

> "This is [the beginning of] what was spoken of through the prophet Joel: 'And it shall be in the last days,' says God, 'that I will pour out My Spirit upon all mankind; and your sons and your daughters shall prophesy, and your young men shall see [divinely prompted] visions, and your old men shall dream [divinely prompted] dreams; even on My bond-servants, both men and women, I will in those days pour out My Spirit and they shall prophesy.'"
>
> Acts 2:16–18 AMP

I announce to you that your season of restoration has begun! Everything in the created order is going to cooperate with you this season! I decree over you that what did not happen in your old season is turning around in this season. It is your time of restoration. Do not miss your season by focusing on past defeats and failures. You are now armed with greater understanding and increased capacity to overcome your enemies. Do not focus on the limitations that many in your family have succumbed to. God is overturning bloodline issues that released curses and limitations over you. God is setting in place a new order and standard in your bloodline, and He is starting with you. This is your season of retribution!

Retribution: The Spoils of War

Remember the law of retribution: Every believer has Kingdom authority to command the release of their captured goods with interest. "A hungry man might steal to fill his stomach. If he is caught, he must pay seven times more than he stole" (Proverbs 6:30–31 ERV). As stated in chapter 9, retribution is a war term referring to release of a portion beyond the portion taken from you. Restoration includes retribution, but too many Kingdom citizens focus only on the lost portion. For too long the focus of Kingdom citizens has been toward restoration or recovery of what was lost. In this season we are to focus on the full scope of what is due to us. This revelation will launch Kingdom citizens into a new dimension of prayer that will activate retribution on our behalf.

When you apprehend the thief stealing your goods, he must pay you up to seven times the amount that was taken from you. Retribution includes losses in your bloodline. Many people have experienced loss in the generations of their families, including wealth, health, broken families, etc. It is time for Kingdom order to be established in your bloodline in a new way. You are entitled to the return of your stuff with interest! This is the principle of multiplication.

Do not be overwhelmed by the size of your enemy. The armies of Israel perceived Goliath as a giant they could not defeat. David saw Goliath as a giant that could not defeat him. David knew that God was on his side! What is your perception of what stands between you and your stuff? Some years ago, a preacher coined the phrase *You can't lose with the stuff I use.*

I want to tell you that when you are moving with heaven, you cannot lose. God has never lost a battle, and He will not start by losing yours. You will take the spoils of war and rescue your children from his attacks.

"Kings will be your attendants, and their princesses your nurses. They will bow down to you with their faces to the earth and lick the dust of your feet; and you shall know [with an understanding based on personal experience] that I am the LORD; for they shall not be put to shame who wait and hope expectantly for Me. Can the spoils of war be taken from the mighty man, or the captives of a tyrant be rescued?" Indeed, this is what the LORD says, "Even the captives of the mighty man will be taken away, and the tyrant's spoils of war will be rescued; for I will contend with your opponent, and I will save your children."

Isaiah 49:23–25 AMP

Now pause and consider how great this man was to whom Abraham, the patriarch, gave a tenth of the spoils.

Hebrews 7:4 AMP

David captured all the flocks and herds [which the enemy had], and [the people] drove those animals before him and said, "This is David's spoil."

1 Samuel 30:20 AMP

Changing the game will require you to begin praying in a new way. Heaven is ready to help you rescue your stuff! Yes, that is right, there is a portion being held captive with your name on it. King David not only recovered his stuff, including his wives and children, he recovered the wives and children of his army and their stuff. Not only that, he took the enemy's stuff! They walked away from the battle singing, "This is David's spoil." It is time for you to sing about the spoil coming to you. There are spoils with your name on it. Some spoils have the names of

165

your family members who are no longer on earth. Even though you do not see it yet, start singing.

|||||||||||||||||||||||||||||||||||||||||||||||||||||||||||||||||||||||||||||||||||||||||||||||||||||||||

Key Scriptures: Numbers 23:19; 1 Chronicles 14; Matthew 7:7; Matthew 4:1–17; Joel 2:25; Acts 2:16–18; Proverbs 6:30–31; Isaiah 49:23–25; 1 Samuel 30:20

Key Points:

- In each war season God will give you strategies for victory. The strategies may change from confrontation to confrontation. Let the Spirit of God order your war movement.
- Be specific in your requests to God. Make a list of needs to fulfill God-given visions.
- Be persistent. God answers prayers.
- Do not die in your wilderness. It is only a temporary stop as you move toward your destination.
- Secure your identity.
- God is establishing a new plumb line in your family, ministry and business.
- Retribution has been an overlooked and neglected aspect of spiritual warfare.

Reflection: In what ways does your identity need to be secured? What new war strategies is the Lord giving to you?

_____

_____

_____

_____

_____

Conclusion

I heard a tremendous praise report from an intercessor who is also a friend. This testimony impacted my faith to believe God for things I thought were difficult, but to God they are not. Several years ago, this intercessor was ministering at a church in south Texas. When the intercessor visited the church, she noticed the town was small, with no major stores or hotels. She described it as "a town emerging."

The host pastor had been a musician prior to surrendering his life to the Lord. After he was saved, wanting to use his instrument to bring glory to God, the pastor would blow his trumpet during worship gatherings. One evening during her visit, the intercessor heard Holy Spirit tell her to give the pastor an instruction: Put the trumpet to the ground and blow. She could not believe what she was hearing and asked Holy Spirit to say it to her again. *Tell him to put his trumpet to the ground and blow*, came the answer. She looked at the pastor and shared with him what she heard Holy Spirit say.

The pastor thought the instruction was ridiculous and was reluctant to blow into the ground. But after a moment or two, he relented; he held his trumpet to the ground and blew. That was it. No earthshaking manifestations. Nothing "appeared" to happen.

They said their good-byes and she traveled back to her city.

One year later, she received a phone call from the pastor. "You have got to come back and see what has happened here!" the pastor exclaimed. "You are not going to believe it!"

The intercessor arranged another visit to the town. What she saw was unbelievable. The town was thriving. Department stores and hotels were being built everywhere. Big oil companies were moving in, spending money and boosting the economy. What had happened? On the very spot the pastor had placed his trumpet to the ground and blew in an act of faith, oil had been discovered. A sound released in obedience to heaven's directive resulted in a shift of the town's entire economy. How did this happen? Both the intercessor and pastor responded in faith and obedience to heaven's directive. The directives God gives you might sound strange, but whenever you obey God's voice, manifestation will occur.

> But God has selected [for His purpose] the foolish things of the world to shame the wise [revealing their ignorance], and God has selected [for His purpose] the weak things of the world to shame the things which are strong [revealing their frailty].
>
> 1 Corinthians 1:27 AMP

> "For My thoughts are not your thoughts, nor are your ways My ways," declares the LORD. "For as the heavens are higher than the earth, so are My ways higher than your ways and My thoughts higher than your thoughts. For as the rain and snow come down from heaven, and do not return there without watering the earth, making it bear and sprout, and providing seed to the sower and bread to the eater, so will My word be which goes out of My mouth; it will not return to Me void (useless,

without result), without accomplishing what I desire, and without succeeding in the matter for which I sent it."

Isaiah 55:8–11 AMP

As you purpose to spend time in prayer, God will make known His strategies to bring you into victory. As it did for Daniel, heaven will move at the sound of your faith-filled words. When heaven moves on your behalf, earth must respond, releasing every blessing timed for this season of your life. Like Daniel, keep pressing in through worship, fasting and prayer. Keep the Word of God in your heart and on your lips. Like Ehud, the left-handed warrior, you will receive from God revelation of how to overcome your enemy. Finally, be like King David; move in God's timing against your enemies. Do not leave any spoils behind—retribution is your portion!

This Book of the Law shall not depart from your mouth, but you shall read [and meditate on] it day and night, so that you may be careful to do [everything] in accordance with all that is written in it; for then you will make your way prosperous, and then you will be successful.

Joshua 1:8 AMP

Notes

Introduction

1. C. Peter Wagner, *Praying with Power: How to Pray Effectively and Clearly* (Shippensburg, Pa.: Destiny Image, 1997), 16.

Chapter 2: Where Did That Come From?

1. We see this in the Greek word *pale*, translated "wrestle" in Ephesians 6:12. *Biblesoft's New Exhaustive Strong's Numbers and Concordance with Expanded Greek-Hebrew Dictionary* (Seattle, Wash.: Biblesoft, Inc., and International Bible Translators, Inc., 2006), No. 3823. (Hereafter "*Strong's Concordance.*")

2. C. Peter Wagner, *Warfare Prayer: What the Bible Says about Spiritual Warfare* (Shippensburg, Pa.: Destiny Image, 2009), 14.

3. Doris M. Wagner, *How to Cast Out Demons: A Guide to the Basics* (Minneapolis: Chosen, 2000), 31.

4. Neela Banerjee, "Wiccans Keep the Faith With a Religion Under Wraps," *New York Times*, May 16, 2007, http://www.nytimes.com/2007/05/16/us/16wiccan.html.

5. Doris Wagner, *Demons*, 23.

6. Barna Group, "Three Spiritual Journeys of Millennials," June 3, 2013, https://www.barna.com/research/three-spiritual-journeys-of-millennials/.

7. C. E. Arnold, "Principalities and Powers," in *The Anchor Yale Bible Dictionary*, ed. David Noel Freedman (New York: Doubleday, 1992), 5:467.

8. Arnold, "Principalities and Powers," 5:467.

9. Arnold, "Principalities and Powers," 5:467.

Chapter 3: Interfering Forces

1. "The Side Effects of Fear," *Daily Devotions* (blog), In Touch Ministries, August 7, 2015, https://www.intouch.org/read/magazine/daily-devotions /the-side-effects-of-fear.
2. Benny Hinn, "7 Things the Anointing Will Do for You," Benny Hinn Ministries, accessed September 5, 2018, https://www.bennyhinn.org/7-things -the-anointing-will-do-for-you.

Chapter 4: Defeating Demonic Carpenters

1. Chuck D. Pierce and Rebecca Sytsema, *The Future War of the Church: How We Can Defeat Lawlessness and Bring God's Order to the Earth* (Minneapolis: Chosen, 2007), 113.
2. Childhood Domestic Violence Association. "10 Startling Statistics about Children of Domestic Violence," February 21, 2014, https://cdv.org/2014/02/10 -startling-domestic-violence-statistics-for-children.
3. National Institute on Alcohol Abuse and Alcoholism, "Children of Alcoholics: Are They Different?" *Alcohol Alert Bulletin*, July 1990, https:// pubs.niaaa.nih.gov/publications/aa09.htm.
4. Chuck D. Pierce and Rebecca Wagner Sytsema, *The Spiritual Warfare Handbook: How to Battle, Pray and Prepare Your House for Triumph* (Grand Rapids: Chosen, 2000), 362.
5. Pierce and Sytsema, *Future War of the Church*, 111.
6. Pierce and Sytsema, *Future War of the Church*, 111–112.
7. *Strong's Concordance*, No. 2032.

Chapter 5: Breaking Cycles of Self-Sabotage

1. Tony Khuon, "11 Subtle Ways You Commit Self-Sabotage Without Knowing it," *Agile Lifestyle*, June 20, 2013, http://agilelifestyle.net/self-sabotage.
2. WebFinance, Inc., "self-fulfilling prophecy," *BusinessDictionary*, accessed October 6, 2018, http://www.businessdictionary.com/definition/self -fulfilling-prophecy.html.

Chapter 6: The Spirit of Pisgah

1. Walter A. Elwell, ed., *Baker Encyclopedia of the Bible* (Grand Rapids: Baker, 1988), 2:1619, s.v. "patience."

Chapter 8: The Power of Faith

1. Chuck D. Pierce and Rebecca Wagner Sytsema, *Prayers That Outwit the Enemy* (Minneapolis: Chosen, 2004), 95.
2. *Strong's Concordance*, No. 3358.
3. Adapted from Pierce and Sytsema, *Prayers That Outwit*, 96.
4. This meaning is present in the Greek word *agnoeō*, translated "ignorant" in 1 Corinthians 12:1. See *Strong's Concordance*, No. 50.

5. Chuck D. Pierce and Robert Heidler, *Restoring Your Shield of Faith* (Minneapolis: Chosen, 2004), 157.

Chapter 10: Armed and Dangerous

1. Myles Munroe, *Understanding Your Place in God's Kingdom: Your Original Purpose for Existence* (Shippensburg, Pa.: Destiny Image, 2001), Kindle edition, 102.
2. *Strong's Concordance*, No. 1849.
3. W. E. Vine, *Vine's Expository Dictionary of Biblical Words*, ed. Merrill Unger and William White (Nashville: Thomas Nelson, 1985), s.v. "authority."
4. Munroe, *Understanding Your Place*, 110.
5. Munroe, *Understanding Your Place*, 158.
6. Munroe, *Understanding Your Place*, 160–165.
7. In Jewish and Christian theology, *Shekinah* is the glory of the divine presence, often represented as light.

Chapter 11: Change the Game!

1. Martin H. Manser, ed., *Dictionary of Bible Themes* (n.p.: BookBaby, 1996), s.v. "7254 plumb-line," https://www.biblegateway.com/resources/dictionary-of-bible-themes/7254-plumb-line.
2. *Strong's Concordance*, No. 7999.

Dr. Venner Alston travels throughout the United States, Europe, the Middle East, Asia, the Caribbean Islands and Africa as an apostle and public speaker. As she ministers, she communicates hope and offers Kingdom solutions to individual and societal issues to both men and women. Venner leads Global Outreach Ministries and Training Center, a thriving ministry in Milwaukee, Wisconsin, and she is also establishing a base for ministry in Texas. Venner has a passion for education and completed her doctoral degree in urban education. She has been a successful entrepreneur, founding and overseeing a preschool program and a private Christian school for fifteen years. Venner Alston is a frequent speaker at Glory of Zion International at the Global Spheres Center, led by Dr. Chuck D. Pierce.

Booking:
Website: www.drvjalston.org
Email: info@drvjalston.org
Facebook: VJ Alston International Ministries (iamdrvjalston)
Twitter: Dr. VJ Alston (iamdrvjalston)
Instagram: Dr. VJ Alston (iamdrvjalston)
Periscope: Dr. VJ Alston (iamdrvjalston)